THE
INDIAN SONG OF SONGS

THE
INDIAN SONG OF SONGS

FROM THE SANSKRIT OF THE GITA GOVINDA

OF JAYADEVA

With other Oriental Poems

EDWIN ARNOLD, M.A., F.R.G.S.

GYAN

Published by

Gyan Publishing House
5, Ansari Road
Daryaganj, New Delhi-110002
Phone: 011-47034999, 9811692060
E-mail: books@gyanbooks.com

Distribution Network
gyanbooks.com
India, USA, Canada, UK, Australia, France

ISBN : 978-81-212-9200-9 (PB)
First Published, 1875

2nd Impression 2023

Printed at: Gyan Press, Delhi.

STHE INDIAN SONG OF SONGS
Author: EDWIN ARNOLD

THE

INDIAN SONG OF SONGS.

FROM THE SANSKRIT OF THE GÎTA GOVINDA OF JAYADEVA.

With other Oriental Poems.

BY

EDWIN ARNOLD, M.A., F.R.G.S.

(OF UNIVERSITY COLL. OXFORD),

FORMERLY PRINCIPAL OF THE POONA COLLEGE, AND FELLOW OF THE UNIVERSITY OF BOMBAY;

Author of "Griselda and other Poems," "Dalhousie's Administration of India," "The Book of Good Counsels," "Hero and Leander," &c. &c.

LONDON:

TRÜBNER & CO., LUDGATE HILL.

1875.

TO

MY MANY HINDOO FRIENDS

IN TOKEN OF

AFFECTIONATE RECOLLECTION.

PREFACE.

Beautiful flowers please, whatever their name and country; and so far as any brightness or frágrance may have been preserved from the Aryan original in this paraphrase, it will no doubt be recognised by the reader of intelligence. Yet being so exotic, the poem demands a word or two of introduction.

The "Gîta Govinda," then, or "Song of Govind," is a Sanskrit idyll, or little pastoral drama, in which—under the form of Krishna, an incarnation of the god Vishnoo—the human soul is displayed in its relations alternately with earthly and celestial beauty. Krishna—at once human and divine—is first seen attracted by the pleasures of the senses (personified by the shepherdesses in the wood), and wasting his affections upon the delights of their illusory world. Radha, the spirit of intellectual and moral beauty, comes to free him from this error by enkindling in his heart a desire for her own surpassing loveliness of form and character; and under the parable of a human passion—too glowingly depicted by the Indian poet for exact transcription —the gradual emancipation of Krishna from sensuous distractions, and his union with Radha in a high and spiritualised happiness, are portrayed. This general interpretation, at any rate, though disputed by certain authorities, is maintained by Jones, Lassen, and others; and has been followed, not without occasional difficulty, in the subjoined version.

Lassen thus writes in his Latin *prolegomena:* "To speak my opinion in one word, Krishna is here the divinely-given soul manifested in humanity. . . . The recollection of this celestial origin abides deep in the mind, and even when it seems to slumber—drugged as it were by the fair shows of the world, the pleasures of visible things, and the intoxication of the senses—it now and again awakes, . . . full of yearning to recover the sweet serenity of its pristine condition. Then the soul begins to discriminate and to perceive that the love, which was its inmost principle, has been lavished on empty and futile objects; it grows a-wearied of things sensual, false, and unenduring; it longs to fix its affection on that which shall be stable, and the source of true and eternal delight. Krishna—to use the imagery of this poem—thrones Radha in his heart, as the sole and only one who can really satisfy his aspirations. . . .

"Radha is supreme in beauty, with a loveliness which is at once celestial, and yet enshrined in earthly mould. Her charms lift the mind to heavenly contemplations, and the God of Love, Kama, borrows his best weapons from them. She is forgiving and pitiful even towards her erring and lingering lover; she would meet him in returning if she could; she grieves more than she blames; and once reconciled, is beyond measure tender. . . . The remedy for the illusions of sense—*sansâra*—is placed by all Hindoo philosophers in the understanding of true existence, and Radha, in my judgment, represents this remedy—being the personified contemplation of the divine beauty and goodness. . . . Such contemplation flies from and disowns the mind possessed by sensual objects, but goes to meet and gladly inhabits that which consecrates itself, as Krishna's does, to the higher love. . . . It bewails its separation from the soul, as that which was its natural dwelling-place before the changeful shows of mortal life banished it; and this is the mystery of mutual attraction between the mind and mental beauty, that the memory of the divine happiness does not die, but is revived by the recognition of truth, and returns to the perception of what things in love are worthless, and what are real and worthy. The affection of Radha is jealous, and grants not the full sight of her charms, until the soul of its own accord abandons its preoccupations, and becomes filled with the desire of the true love. But upon the soul thus returning she lavishes her utmost tenderness; whereof to be the recipient is to have all wishes fulfilled and nothing lacking —to be *tripta*—'well-contented.' Such, in my opinion, is the recondite significance of this poem, hidden under imagery but too luxuriant. The Indian poet seems, indeed, to have spent rather more labour in depicting the phases of earthly passion than of that intellectual yearning by which the mind is lifted to the contemplation of divine things; . . . but the fable of the loves of Govinda and Radha existing from antiquity, and being universally accepted, philosophy had to affix its doctrines to the story in such a way as that the vulgar amours of those popular deities might present themselves in a nobler aspect."

Nothing in the way of exposition needs to be added to these words.

The great variety of measure in the original has been indicated by frequently varying the metre of this paraphrase, without meanwhile attempting to imitate the many very fanciful alliterations, assonances, and recurring choruses; of which last, however, two examples have been introduced. The "Gîta Govinda," with these *refrains* and the musical accompaniments named and prescribed by the directions embodied in the text, must have been a species of Oriental opera. This raises the difficult and little-studied subject of ancient Hindoo music, upon which a passing word or two may not appear impertinent. Sir William Jones says, "When I first read the songs of Jayadeva, who has prefixed to each the name of the mode in which it was to be sung, I had hopes of procuring the original music; but the Pundits of the South referred me to those of the West, and the Brahmans of the West would have sent me to those of the North, while they of Nepal and Cashmere declared that they had no ancient music, but imagined that the notes of the "Gîta Govinda" must exist, if anywhere, where the poet was born" (Sir W. Jones, vol. i. p. 440).

Now the reason why this illustrious scholar could not find the score of the "Gîta," was that music was always taught orally by the Hindoos, and therefore did not pass down from the old minstrels in any noted form. Yet there existed an elaborate science of melody among the ancient Indians; although, like the Greeks, they understood little or nothing of harmony. The distinguishing feature of Hindoo airs was, and still is, an extremely fine gradation of notes; the semitone could be accurately divided into demi-semitones by the ear and voice of a practised "Gundharb" or "Goonee." This even now imparts a delicacy to the otherwise monotonous temple-singing, which all musicians would recognise; and they might find in such treatises as the "Sungeet Durpun," "Ragavibodha," and "Râg-mala," or "Chaplet of Melodies," complete and curious explanations of the Hindoo orchestra. In that fantastic system the old Aryan composers established six *ragas*, or divine fundamental airs, having each five wives or *raginees*, and each of these producing eight melodious children; so that the orthodox repertory contained two hundred and forty separate songs. These songs had their fixed occasion, subject, and season; all to be reverently observed; otherwise the deity presiding over each was not thought likely to attend and give perfect effect to the music. These lyric divinities are personified and described in such works as the "Ratnamala:" thus "Gurjjarî"—a melody frequently indicated here by Jayadeva—is represented as a feminine minstrel of engaging mien, dressed in yellow bodice and red *saree*, richly bedecked with jewels and enthroned in a golden swing, as the third wife of the *Raga Megh*. Musical science was divided into seven branches—*Surudhyaya* or sol-fa-ing, *rag* or melody, *tal* or time, *nrit* or rhythmical dancing, *aurth* or poetry, *bhav* or expression, and *hust*, answering to method, "touch." The gamut contained seven notes singularly named—*Su* was *suruj*, the scream of the peacock; *ri* was *rikhub*, the cry of the parrot; *gu* was *gundhur*, the bleat of the sheep; *mu* was *muddhun*, the call of the crane; *pu* stood for *punchum*, and the note of the Koïl; *dhu* for *dhyvut*, the neigh of the horse; and *ni* for *nikhad*, the trumpeting of the elephant. Endless subtleties characterised their musical terms—thus *tal*, or "time," is a word made up of the first letters from *tand*, the dance of Mahadeo, and *las*, the dance of Parvati, his consort; but these are mere etymological niceties, characteristic of the hard language in which one single word may be written in a hundred and eight ways. Enough has been said to show, from sources which are perhaps somewhat out of general reach, that a special accompaniment of music was prescribed for the "Gîta Govinda" when composed, which, could it be recovered, would add immensely to the interest of the Sanskrit Canticle; and indeed, even at present, any competent inquirer into the existing melodies of India, popular and sacred, might be rewarded by many exquisite airs worth the ear of European *maestri* themselves. The Indians of to-day have still their *dhoorpuds*, or heroic ballads; their *kheals*, *ghuzuls*, and *rekhtahs*, love-songs of Mogul derivation; their *dadras* and *nuktas*, serenades of Hindoo origin; the *tuppah*, hummed by Hindi and Punjabi camel-drivers; the *terana*, or "song without words;" the *palna*, or cradle-song; the *sohla*, or marriage-strain; the *stooti*, or eulogistic chants; and the *zikri*, which are hymns of morality. Probably among these some echoes of the antique melodies of Jayadeva may be preserved; at any rate, such a list—and it might be largely extended—shows that Indian music well merits professional study.

Jayadeva, a native of Kinduvilva or Kendôli, in Burdwan or Tirhoot (for the locality is doubtful), wrote, according to Lassen, about 1150 A.D. The theme of the Indian poet's musical mystery-play is found in the tenth section of the Bhâgavata, but Hindoo literature and daily talk are full of this half-divine, half-human Krishna; and in turning into a religious canticle the loves of "Govinda" and Radha, Jayadeva might be sure that every native audience, present and to come, would understand his matter. The "Gîta" is to this hour very popular in India; but more so, doubtless, because of its melodious versification and its ardent love-pictures than the profound and earnest meanings, for the sake of which this imperfect attempt has been hazarded. Extremely imperfect it is, and for exact Sanskrit scholars (among whose honourable number the Author has very slender claims to rank) of no account at all; yet something, however slight, may perhaps be done towards the closer acquaintance of England and India—an object always dear to the present writer—by this his second effort to popularise Indian classics. With the aid of Lassen (to whose labours and erudite guidance every grateful acknowledgment is here due) this "Song of Songs" goes, for the most part, fairly pace for pace with the Sanskrit text; although much has had to be modified, and the last Sarga omitted, in order to comply with the canons of Western propriety. An English dress cannot—alas!—fail to destroy something of the Asiatic grace of Radha; but in her own she is radiant, fascinating, and angelic, and seemed to teach a lesson so well worth repeating, that this imitation of Jayadeva has been ventured upon.

LONDON, *August* 1875.

CONTENTS.

INTRODUCTION.

SARGA THE FIRST.

SARGA THE SECOND.

SARGA THE THIRD.

SARGA THE FOURTH.

SARGA THE FIFTH.

SARGA THE SIXTH.

SARGA THE SEVENTH.

SARGA THE EIGHTH.

SARGA THE NINTH.

SARGA THE TENTH.

SARGA THE ELEVENTH.

THE INDIAN SONG OF SONGS.

INTRODUCTION.

OM!

REVERENCE TO GANESHA!

"THE sky is clouded; and the wood resembles
The sky, thick-arched with black Tamâla boughs;
O Radha, Radha! take this Soul, that trembles
In life's deep midnight, to Thy golden house."
So Nanda spoke,—and, led by Radha's spirit,
The feet of Krishna found the road aright;
Wherefore in bliss which all high hearts inherit
Together taste they Love's divine delight.

He who wrote these things for thee,
Of the Son of Wassoodee,
Was the poet Jayadeva;
Him Saraswati gave ever
Fancies fair his mind to throng,
Like pictures palace-walls along;
Ever to his notes of love
Lakshmi's mystic dancers move.
If thy spirit seeks to brood
On Hari glorious, Hari good;
If it feeds on solemn numbers
Dim as dreams and soft as slumbers,
Lend thine ear to Jayadev,
Lord of all the spells that save.
Umapatidhara's strain
Glows like roses after rain;
Sharan's stream-like song is grand,
If its tide ye understand;
Bard more wise beneath the sun
Is not found than Govardhun;
Dhoyi holds the listener still
With his shlokes of subtle skill;

But for sweet words suited well
Jayadeva doth excel.

(*What follows is to the Music* Mâlava *and the Mode* Rupaka.)

HYMN TO VISHNU.

O thou that held'st the blessed Veda dry
When all things else beneath the floods were hurled;
Strong Fish-God! Ark of Men! *Jai! Hari, jai!*
Hail, Keshav, hail! thou Master of the world!

The round world rested on thy spacious nape;
Upon thy neck, like a mere mole, it stood:
O thou that took'st for us the Tortoise-shape,
Hail, Keshav, hail! Ruler of wave and wood!

The world upon thy curving tusk sate sure,
Like the Moon's dark disc in her crescent pale;
O thou who didst for us assume the Boar,
Immortal Conqueror! hail, Keshav, hail!

When thou thy Giant-Foe didst seize and rend,
  Fierce, fearful, long, and sharp were fang and nail;
Thou who the Lion and the Man didst blend,
  Lord of the Universe! hail, Narsingh, hail!

Wonderful Dwarf!—who with a threefold stride
  Cheated King Bali—where thy footsteps fall
Men's sins, O Wamuna! are set aside.
  O Keshev, hail! thou Help and Hope of all!

The sins of this sad earth thou didst assoil,
  The anguish of its creatures thou didst heal;
Freed are we from all terrors by thy toil:
  Hail, Purshuram, hail! Lord of the biting steel!

To thee the fell Ten-Headed yielded life,
  Thou in dread battle laid'st the monster low!
Ah, Rama! dear to Gods and men that strife;
  We praise thee, Master of the matchless bow!

With clouds for garments glorious thou dost fare,
  Veiling thy dazzling majesty and might,
As when Yamuna saw thee with the share,
  A peasant—yet the King of Day and Night.

Merciful-hearted! when thou camest as Boodh—
  Albeit 'twas written in the Scriptures so—
Thou bad'st our altars be no more imbrued
  With blood of victims: Keshav! bending low

We praise thee, Wielder of the sweeping sword,
  Brilliant as curving comets in the gloom,
Whose keen edge smote the fierce barbarian horde;
  Hail to thee, Keshav! hail, and hear, and come,

And fill this song of Jayadev with thee,
  And make it wise to teach, strong to redeem,
And sweet to living souls. Thou Mystery!
  Thou Light of Life! Thou Dawn beyond the dream!

Fish! that didst outswim the flood;
Tortoise! whereon earth hath stood;
Boar! who with thy tush held'st high
The world, that mortals might not die;
Lion! who hast giants torn;
Dwarf! who laugh'dst a king to scorn;
Sole Subduer of the Dreaded!
Slayer of the many-headed!

Mighty Ploughman! Teacher tender!
Of thine own the sure Defender!
Under all thy ten disguises
Endless praise to thee arises.

(*What follows is to the Music* GURJJARÎ *and the Mode* NIHSÂRA.)

Endless praise arises,
O thou God that liest
Rapt, on Kumla's breast,
Happiest, holiest, highest!
Planets are thy jewels,
Stars thy forehead-gems,
Set like sapphires gleaming
In kingliest anadems;
Even the great gold Sun-God,
Blazing through the sky,
Serves thee but for crest-stone,
Jai, jai! Hari, *jai!*
As that Lord of day
After night brings morrow,
Thou dost charm away
Life's long dream of sorrow.

As on Mansa's water
Brood the swans at rest,
So thy laws sit stately
On a holy breast.
O, Drinker of the poison!
Ah, high Delight of earth!
What light is to the lotus-buds,
What singing is to mirth,
Art thou—art thou that slayedst
Madhou and Narak grim;
That ridest on the King of Birds,
Making all glories dim.
With eyes like open lotus-flowers,
Bright in the morning rain,
Freeing by one swift piteous glance
The spirit from Life's pain:
Of all the three Worlds Treasure!
Of sin the Putter-by!
Of the Ten-Headed Victor!
Jai Hari! Hari! *jai!*
Thou Shaker of the Mountain!
Thou Shadow of the Storm!

Thou Cloud that unto Lakshmi's face
Comes welcome, white, and warm!
O thou,—who to great Lakshmi
Art like the silvery beam
Which moon-sick chakors feed upon
By Jumna's silent stream,—
To thee this hymn ascendeth,
That Jayadev doth sing,
Of worship, love, and mystery;
High Lord and heavenly King!
And unto whoso hears it
Do thou a blessing bring—
Whose neck is gilt with yellow dust
From lilies that did cling
Beneath the breasts of Lakshmi,
A girdle soft and sweet,
When in divine embracing
The lips of Gods did meet;
And the beating heart above
Of thee—Dread Lord of Heaven!—
She left that stamp of love—
By such deep sign be given

Prays Jayadev, the glory
And the secret and the spells
Which close-hid in this story
Unto wise ears he tells.

END OF INTRODUCTION.

SARGA THE FIRST.

SAMODADAMODARO.

THE SPORTS OF KRISHNA.

BEAUTIFUL Radha, jasmine-bosomed Radha,
All in the spring-time waited by the wood
For Krishna fair, Krishna the all-forgetful,—
Krishna with earthly love's false fire consuming—
And some one of her maidens sang this song:—

(*What follows is to the Music* VASANTA *and the Mode* YATI.)

I know where Krishna tarries in these early days of
Spring,
When every wind from warm Malay brings fragrance
on its wing;

Brings fragrance stolen far away from thickets of the clove,
In jungles where the bees hum and the Koïl flutes her love;
He dances with the dancers, of a merry morrice one,
All in the budding Spring-time, for 'tis sad to be alone.

I know how Krishna passes these hours of blue and gold,
When parted lovers sigh to meet and greet and closely hold
Hand fast in hand; and every branch upon the Vakul-tree
Droops downward with a hundred blooms, in every bloom a bee;
He is dancing with the dancers to a laughter-moving tone,
In the soft awakening Spring-time, when 'tis hard to live alone.

Where Kroona-flowers, that open at a lover's lightest
tread,
Break, and, for shame at what they hear, from white
blush modest red;
And all the spears on all the boughs of all the Ketuk-
glades
Seem ready darts to pierce the hearts of wandering
youths and maids;
'Tis there thy Krishna dances till the merry drum is done,
All in the sunny Spring-time, when who can live alone?

Where the breaking-forth of blossom on the yellow
Keshra-sprays
Dazzles like Kama's sceptre, whom all the world obeys;
And Pâtal-buds fill drowsy bees from pink delicious
bowls,
As Kama's nectared goblet steeps in languor human
souls;
There he dances with the dancers, and of Radha thinketh
none,
All in the warm new Spring-tide, when none will live
alone.

Where the breath of waving Mâdhvi pours incense
through the grove,
And silken Mogras lull the sense with essences of
love,—
The silken-soft pale Mogra, whose perfume fine and
faint
Can melt the coldness of a maid, the sternness of a
saint—
There dances with those dancers thine other self, thine
Own,
All in the languorous Spring-time, when none will live
alone.

Where—as if warm lips touched sealed eyes and waked
them—all the bloom
Opens upon the mangoes to feel the sunshine
come;
And Atimuktas wind their arms of softest green
about,
Clasping the stems, while calm and clear great Jumna
spreadeth out;

There dances and there laughs thy Love, with damsels
many an one,
In the rosy days of Spring-time, for he will not live alone.

Mark this song of Jayadev!
Deep as pearl in ocean-wave
Lurketh in its lines a wonder
Which the wise alone will ponder:
Though it seemeth of the earth,
Heavenly is the music's birth;
Telling darkly of delights
In the wood, of wasted nights,
Of witless days, and fruitless love,
And false pleasures of the grove,
And rash passions of the prime,
And those dances of Spring-time;
Time, which seems so subtle-sweet,
Time, which pipes to dancing-feet,
Ah! so softly—ah! so sweetly—
That among those wood-maids featly
Krishna cannot choose but dance,
Letting pass life's greater chance.

Yet the winds that sigh so
  As they stir the rose,
Wake a sigh from Krishna
  Wistfuller than those;
All their faint breaths swinging
  The creepers to and fro
Pass like rustling arrows
  Shot from Kama's bow:
Thus among the dancers
  What those zephyrs bring
Strikes to Krishna's spirit
  Like a darted sting.

And all as if—far wandered—
  The traveller should hear
The bird of home, the Koïl,
  With nest-notes rich and clear;
And there should come one moment
  A blessed fleeting dream
Of the bees among the mangoes
  Beside his native stream;

So flash those sudden yearnings,
That sense of a dearer thing,
The love and lack of Radha
Upon his soul in Spring.

Then she, the maid of Radha, spake again;
And pointing far away between the leaves
Guided her lovely Mistress where to look,
And note how Krishna wantoned in the wood
Now with this one, now that; his heart, her prize,
Panting with foolish passions, and his eyes
Beaming with too much love for those fair girls—
Fair, but not so as Radha; and she sang

(*What follows is to the Music* RÂMAGIRÎ *and the Mode* YATI.)

See, Lady! how thy Krishna passes these idle hours
Decked forth in fold of woven gold, and crowned with forest-flowers;

And scented with the sandal, and gay with gems of
price—
Rubies to mate his laughing lips, and diamonds like his
eyes;—
In the company of damsels,* who dance and sing and
play,
Lies Krishna laughing, toying, dreaming his Spring away.

One, with star-blossomed champâk wreathed, woos him
to rest his head
On the dark pillow of her breast so tenderly outspread;
And o'er his brow with roses blown she fans a fragrance
rare,
That falls on the enchanted sense like rain in thirsty
air,
While the company of damsels wave many an odorous
spray,
And Krishna laughing, toying, sighs the soft Spring
away.

---

* It will be observed that the "Gopis" here personify the five senses. Lassen says, "*Manifestum est puellis istis nil aliud significari quam res sensiles.*"

Another, gazing in his face, sits wistfully apart,
Searching it with those looks of love that leap from heart to heart;
Her eyes—afire with shy desire, veiled by their lashes black—
Speak so that Krishna cannot choose but send the message back,
In the company of damsels whose bright eyes in a ring
Shine round him with soft meanings in the merry light of Spring.

The third one of that dazzling band of dwellers in the wood—
Body and bosom panting with the pulse of youthful blood—
Leans over him, as in his ear a lightsome thing to speak,
And then with leaf-soft lip imprints a kiss below his cheek;
A kiss that thrills, and Krishna turns at the silken touch
To give it back—ah, Radha! forgetting thee too much.

And one with arch smile beckons him away from
Jumna's banks,
Where the tall bamboos bristle like spears in battle-
ranks,
And plucks his cloth to make him come into the mango-
shade,
Where the fruit is ripe and golden, and the milk and
cakes are laid:
Oh! golden-red the mangoes, and glad the feasts of
Spring,
And fair the flowers to lie upon, and sweet the dancers
sing.

Sweetest of all that Temptress who dances for him
now
With subtle feet which part and meet in the Râs-
measure slow,
To the chime of silver bangles and the beat of rose-leaf
hands,
And pipe and lute and cymbal played by the woodland
bands;

So that wholly passion-laden—eye, ear, sense, soul
o'ercome—
Krishna is theirs in the forest; his heart forgets its
home.

Krishna, made for heavenly things,
'Midst those woodland singers sings;
With those dancers dances featly,
Gives back soft embraces sweetly;
Smiles on that one, toys with this,
Glance for glance and kiss for kiss;
Meets the merry damsels fairly,
Plays the round of folly rarely,
Lapped in milk-warm spring-time weather,
He and those brown girls together.

And this shadowed earthly love
In the twilight of the grove,
Dance and song and soft caresses,
Meeting looks and tangled tresses,
Jayadev the same hath writ,
That ye might have gain of it,

Sagely its deep sense conceiving
And its inner light believing;
How that Love—the mighty Master,
Lord of all the stars that cluster
In the sky, swiftest and slowest,
Lord of highest, Lord of lowest—
Manifests himself to mortals,
Winning them toward the portals
Of his secret House, the gates
Of that bright Paradise which waits
The wise in love. Ah, human creatures!
Even your phantasies are teachers.
Mighty Love makes sweet in seeming
Even Krishna's woodland dreaming;
Mighty love sways all alike
From self to selflessness. Oh! strike
From your eyes the veil, and see
What Love willeth him to be
Who in error, but in grace,
Sitteth with that lotus-face,
And those eyes whose rays of heaven
Unto phantom-eyes are given;

Holding feasts of foolish mirth
With these Visions of the earth;
Learning love, and love imparting;
Yet with sense of loss upstarting,—

For the cloud that veils the fountains
Underneath the Sandal mountains,
How—as if the sunshine drew
All its being to the blue—
It takes flight, and seeks to rise
High into the purer skies,
High into the snow and frost,
On the shining summits lost!
Ah! and how the Koïls' strain
Smites the traveller with pain,—
When the mango blooms in spring,
And "Koohoo," "Koohoo," they sing—
Pain of pleasures not yet won,
Pain of journeys not yet done,
Pain of toiling without gaining,
Pain, 'mid gladness, of still paining.

But may He guide us all to glory high
Who laughed when Radha glided, hidden, by,
And all among those damsels free and bold
Touched Krishna with a soft mouth, kind and cold;
And like the others, leaning on his breast,
Unlike the others, left there Love's unrest;
And like the others, joining in his song,
Unlike the others, made him silent long.

(*Here ends that Sarga of the Gîta Govinda entitled*
SAMODADAMODARO.)

SARGA THE SECOND.

KLESHAKESHAVO.

THE PENITENCE OF KRISHNA.

THUS lingered Krishna in the deep, green wood,
And gave himself, too prodigal, to those;
But Radha, heart-sick at his falling-off,
Seeing her heavenly beauty slighted so,
Withdrew; and, in a bower of Paradise—
Where nectarous blossoms wove a shrine of shade,
Haunted by birds and bees of unknown skies—
She sate deep-sorrowful, and sang this strain,

(*What follows is to the Music* GURJJARÎ *and the Mode* YATI.)

Ah, my Beloved! taken with those glances,
Ah, my Beloved! dancing those rash dances,
  Ah, Minstrel! playing wrongful strains so well;

Ah, Krishna! Krishna, with the honeyed lip!
Ah, Wanderer into foolish fellowship!
  My Dancer, my Delight!—I love thee still.

O Dancer! strip thy peacock-crown away,
Rise! thou whose forehead is the star of day,
  With beauty for its silver halo set;
Come! thou whose greatness gleams beneath its
    shroud
Like Indra's rainbow shining through the cloud—
  Come, for I love thee, my Beloved! yet.

Must love thee—cannot choose but love thee ever,
My best Beloved—set on this endeavour,
  To win thy tender heart and earnest eye
From lips but sadly sweet, from restless bosoms,
To mine, O Krishna with the mouth of blossoms!
  To mine, thou soul of Krishna! yet I sigh

Half hopeless, thinking of myself forsaken,
And thee, dear Loiterer, in the wood o'ertaken
  With passion for those bold and wanton ones,

Who knit thine arms as poison-plants gripe trees
With twining cords—their flowers the braveries
That flash in the green gloom, sparkling gauds and
stones.

My Prince! my Lotus-faced! my woe! my love!
Whose broad brow, with the tilka-mark above,
Shames the bright moon at full with fleck of cloud;
Thou to mistake so little for so much!
Thou, Krishna, to be palm to palm with such!
O Soul made for my joys, pure, perfect, proud!

Ah, my Beloved! in thy darkness dear;
Ah, Dancer! with the jewels in thine ear,
Swinging to music of a loveless love;
O my Beloved! in thy fall so high
That angels, sages, spirits of the sky
Linger about thee, watching in the grove.

I will be patient still, and draw thee ever,
My one Beloved, sitting by the river
Under the thick Kadambas with that throng:

Will there not come an end to earthly madness?
Shall I not, past the sorrow, have the gladness?
Must not the love-light shine for him ere long?

Shine, thou Light by Radha given,
Shine, thou splendid star of heaven!
Be a lamp to Krishna's feet,
Show to all hearts secrets sweet,
Of the wonder and the love
Jayadev hath writ above.
Be the quick Interpreter
Unto wisest ears of her
Who always sings to all, "I wait,
He loveth still who loveth late."

For (sang on that high Lady in the shade)
My soul for tenderness, not blame, was made;
Mine eyes look through his evil to his good;
My heart coins pleas for him; my fervent thought
Prevents what he will say when these are naught,
And that which I am shall be understood.

Then spake she to her maiden wistfully—

(*What follows is to the Music* MÂLAVAGAUDA *and the Mode* EKATÂLÎ.)

Go to him,—win him hither,—whisper low
  How he may find me if he searches well;
Say, if he will—joys past his hope to know
  Await him here; go now to him, and tell
Where Radha is, and that henceforth she charms
          His spirit to her arms.

Yes, go! say, if he will, that he may come—
  May come, my love, my longing, my desire;
May come forgiven, shriven, to me his home,
  And make his happy peace; nay, and aspire
To uplift Radha's veil, and learn at length
          What love is in its strength.

Lead him; say softly I shall chide his blindness,
  And vex him with my angers; yet add this,
He shall not vainly sue for loving-kindness,
  Nor miss to see me close, nor lose the bliss
That lives upon my lip, nor be denied
          The rose-throne at my side.

Say that I—Radha—in my bower languish
  All widowed, till he find the way to me;
Say that mine eyes are dim, my breast all anguish,
  Until with gentle murmured shame I see
His steps come near, his anxious pleading face
            Bend for my pardoning grace.

While I—what, did he deem light loves so tender,
  To tarry for them when the vow was made,
To yield him up my bosom's maiden splendour,
  And fold him in my fragrance, and unbraid
My shining hair for him, and clasp him close
            To the gold heart of his Rose,

And sing him strains which only spirits know,
  And make him captive with the silk-soft chain
Of twinned-wings brooding round him, and bestow
  Kisses of Paradise, as pure as rain;
My gems, my moonlight-pearls, my girdle-gold,
            Cymbaling music bold?

While gained for ever, I shall dare to grow
  Life to life with him, in the realms divine ;
And—Love's large cup at happy overflow,
  Yet ever to be filled—his eyes and mine
Shall meet in that glad look, when Time's great gate
          Closes and shuts out Fate.

Listen to the unsaid things
Of the song which Radha sings,
For the soul draws near to bliss,
As it comprehendeth this.
I am Jayadev, who write
All this subtle-rich delight
For your teaching. Ponder, then,
What it tells to Gods and men.
Err not, watching Krishna gay,
With those brown girls all at play ;
Understand how Radha charms
Her wandering lover to her arms.
Waiting with divinest love
Till his dream ends in the grove.

For even now (she sang) I see him pause,
  Heart-stricken with the waste of heart he makes
Amid them ;—all the bows of their bent brows
  Wound him no more : no more for all their sakes
Plays he one note upon his amorous lute,
          But lets the strings lie mute.

Pensive, as if his parted lips should say—

"My feet with the dances are weary,
  The music has dropped from the song,
There is no more delight in the lute-strings,
  Sweet Shadows ! what thing has gone wrong ?
The wings of the wind have left fanning
  The palms of the glade ;
They are dead, and the blossoms seem dying
  In the place where we played.

"We will play no more, beautiful Shadows !
  A fancy came solemn and sad,
More sweet, with unspeakable longings,
  Than the best of the pleasures we had :

I am not now the Krishna who kissed you;
That exquisite dream,—
The Vision I saw in my dancing—
Has spoiled what you seem.

"Ah! delicate phantoms that cheated
With eyes that looked lasting and true,
I awake,—I have seen her,—my angel—
Farewell to the wood and to you!
Oh, whisper of wonderful pity!
Oh, fair face that shone!
Though thou be a vision, Divinest!
This vision is done."

(*Here ends that Sarga of the Gîta Govinda entitled* KLESHAKESHAVO.)

SARGA THE THIRD.

MUGDHAMADHUSUDANO.

KRISHNA TROUBLED.

THEREAT,—as one who welcomes to her throne
A new-made Queen, and brings before it bound
Her enemies,—so Krishna in his heart
Throned Radha; and—all treasonous follies chained—
He played no more with those first play-fellows:
But, searching through the shadows of the grove
For loveliest Radha,—when he found her not,
Faint with the quest, despairing, lonely, lorn,
And pierced with shame for wasted love and days,

He satc by Jumna, where the canes are thick,
And sang to the wood-echoes words like these:

(*What follows is to the Music* GURJJARI *and the Mode* YATI.)

Radha, Enchantress! Radha, queen of all!
  Gone—lost, because she found me sinning here;
And I so stricken with my foolish fall,
  I could not stay her out of shame and fear;
                She will not hear;
In her disdain and grief vainly I call.

And if she heard, what would she do? what say?
  How could I make it good that I forgot?
What profit was it to me, night and day,
  To live, love, dance, and dream, having her not?
                Soul without spot!
I wronged thy patience, till it sighed away.

Sadly I see the truth. Ah! even now
  Remembering that one look beside the river,

Softter the vexed eyes seem, and the proud brow
  Than lotus-leaves when the bees make them quiver.
                    My love for ever!
Too late is Krishna wise—too far art thou!

Yet all day long in my deep heart I woo thee,
  And all night long with thee my dreams are sweet;
Why, then, so vainly must my steps pursue thee?
  Why can I never reach thee to entreat,
                    Low at thy feet,
Dear vanished Splendour! till my tears subdue thee?

Surpassing Oue! I knew thou didst not brook
  Half-hearted worship, and a love that wavers;
Haho! there is the wisdom I mistook,
  Therefore I seek with desperate endeavours;
                    That fault dissevers
Me from my heaven, astray—condemned—forsook!

And yet I seem to feel, to know, thee near me;
  Thy steps make music, measured music, near;

Radha! my Radha! will not sorrow clear me?
Shine once! speak one word pitiful and dear!
Wilt thou not hear?
Canst thou—because I did forget—forsake me?

Forgive! the sin is sinned, is past, is over;
No thought I think shall do thee wrong again;
Turn thy dark eyes again upon thy lover,
Bright Spirit! or I perish of this pain.
Loving again!
In dread of doom to love, but not recover.

So did Krishna sing and sigh
By the river-bank; and I,
Jayadev of Kinduvilva,
Resting—as the moon of silver
Sits upon the solemn ocean—
On full faith in deep devotion;
Tell it that ye may perceive
How the heart must fret and grieve;
How the soul doth tire of earth,
When the love from Heav'n hath birth.

For (sang he on) I am no foe of thine,
  There is no black snake, Kama! in my hair;
Blue lotus-leaves, and not the poisoned brine,
  Shadow my neck; what stains my bosom bare,
            Thou God unfair!
Is sandal-dust, not ashes; nought of mine

Makes me like Shiva that thou, Lord of Love!
  Shouldst strain thy string at me and fit thy dart;
This world is thine—let be one breast thereof
  Which bleeds already, wounded to the heart
            With lasting smart,
Shot from those brows that did my sin reprove.

Thou gavest her those black brows for a bow
  Arched like thine own, whose pointed arrows
      seem
Her glances, and the underlids that go—
  So firm and fine—its string? Ah, fleeting gleam!
            Beautiful dream!
Small need of Kama's help hast thou, I trow,

To smite me to the soul with love;—but set
  Those arrows to their silken cord! enchain
My thoughts in that loose hair! let thy lips, wet
  With dew of heaven as bimba-buds with rain,
          Bloom precious pain
Of longing in my heart; and, keener yet,

The heaving of thy lovely, angry bosom,
  Pant to my spirit things unseen, unsaid;
But if thy touch, thy tones, if the dark blossom
  Of thy dear face, thy jasmine-odours shed
          From feet to head,
If these be all with me, canst thou be far—be fled?

So sang he, and I pray that whoso hears
The music of his burning hopes and fears,
That whoso sees this vision by the River
Of Krishna, Hari, (can we name him ever?)
And marks his ear-ring rubies swinging slow,
As he sits still, unheedful, bending low
To play this tune upon his lute, while all
Listen to catch the sadness musical;

And Krishna wotteth nought, but with set face
Turned full toward Radha's plays on in that place;
May all such souls—prays Jayadev—be wise
To learn the wisdom which hereunder lies.

(*Here ends that Sarga of the Gîta Govinda entitled*
MUGDHAMADHUSUDANO.)

SARGA THE FOURTH.

SNIGDHAMADHUSUDANO.

KRISHNA CHEERED.

THEN she whom Radha sent came to the canes—
The canes beside the river where he lay
With listless limbs and spirit weak from love;—
And she sang this to Krishna wistfully.

(*What follows is to the Music* KARNÂTA *and the Mode* EKATÂLÎ.)

Art thou sick for Radha? she is sad in turn,
  Heaven foregoes its blessings, if it holds not thee;
All the cooling fragrance of sandal she doth spurn,
  Moonlight makes her mournful with radiance silvery;

Even the southern breeze blown fresh from pearly seas,
  Seems to her but tainted by a dolorous brine;
And for thy sake discontented, with a great love overladen,
  Her soul comes here beside thee, and sitteth down with thine.

Her soul comes here beside thee, and tenderly and true
  It weaves a subtle mail of proof to ward off sin and pain;
A breastplate soft as lotus-leaf, with holy tears for dew,
  To guard thee from the things that hurt; and then 'tis gone again
To strew a blissful place with the richest buds that grace
  Kama's sweet world, a meeting-spot with rose and jasmine fair,
For the hour when, well-contented, with a love no longer troubled,
  Thou shalt find the way to Radha, and finish sorrows there.

But now her lovely face is shadowed by her fears;
Her glorious eyes are veiled and dim like moonlight in eclipse
By breaking rain-clouds, Krishna! yet she paints you in her tears
With tender thoughts—not Krishna, but brow and breast and lips
And form and mien a King, a great and god-like thing;
And then with bended head she asks grace from the Love Divine,
To keep thee discontented with the phantoms thou forswearest,
Till she may win her glory, and thou be raised to thine.

Softly now she sayeth,
"Krishna, Krishna, come!"
Lovingly she prayeth,
"Fair moon, light him home."
Yet if Hari helps not,
Moonlight cannot aid;
Ah! the woeful Radha!
Ah! the forest shade!

Ah! if Hari guide not,
  Moonlight is as gloom;
Ah! if moonlight help not,
  How shall Krishna come?
Sad for Krishna grieving
  In the darkened grove;
Sad for Radha weaving
  Dreams of fruitless love!

Strike soft strings to this soft measure,
If thine ear would catch its treasure;
Slowly dance to this deep song,
Let its meaning float along
With grave paces, since it tells
Of a love that sweetly dwells
In a tender distant glory,
Past all faults of mortal story.

(*What follows is to the Music* DESHÂGA *and the Mode* EKATÂLÎ.)

Krishna, till thou come unto her, faint she lies with love and fear;
Even the jewels of her necklet seem a load too great to bear.

Krishna, till thou come unto her, all the sandal and the flowers
Vex her with their pure perfection though they grow in heavenly bowers.

Krishna, till thou come unto her, fair albeit those bowers may be,
Passion burns her, and love's fire fevers her for lack of thee.

Krishna, till thou come unto her, those divine lids, dark and tender,
Droop like lotus-leaves in rain-storms, dashed and heavy in their splendour.

Krishna, till thou come unto her, that rose-couch which
she hath spread
Saddens with its empty place, its double pillow for one
head.

Krishna, till thou come unto her, from her palms she
will not lift
The dark face hidden deep within them like the moon
in cloudy rift.

Krishna, till thou come unto her, angel though she be,
thy Love
Sighs and suffers, waits and watches—joyless 'mid those
joys above.

Krishna, till thou come unto her, with the comfort of
thy kiss
Deeper than thy loss, O Krishna! must be loss of
Radha's bliss.

Krishna, while thou didst forget her—her, thy life, thy
gentle fate—
Wonderful her waiting was, her pity sweet, her
patience great.

Krishna, come! 'tis grief untold to grieve her—shame to let her sigh;
Come, for she is sick with love, and thou her only remedy.

So she sang, and Jayadeva
Prays for all, and prays for ever,
That Great Hari may bestow
Utmost bliss of loving so
On us all;—that one who wore
The herdsman's form, and heretofore,
To save the shepherd's threatened flock,
Up from the earth reared the huge rock—
Bestow it with a gracious hand,
Albeit, amid the woodland band,
Clinging close in fond caresses
Krishna gave them ardent kisses.
Taking on his lips divine
Earthly stamp and woodland sign.

(*Here ends that Sarga of the Gîta Govinda entitled*
SNIGDHAMADHUSUDANO.)

SARGA THE FIFTH.

SAKANDKSHAPUNDARIKAKSHO.

THE LONGINGS OF KRISHNA.

"SAY I am here! oh, if she pardons me,
Say where I am, and win her softly hither,"
So Krishna to the maid; and willingly
She came again to Radha, and she sang

(*What follows is to the Music* DESHIVARÂDÎ *and the Mode* RUPAKA.)

Low whispers the wind from Malaya
O'erladen with love;
On the hills all the grass is burned yellow;
And the trees in the grove

Droop with tendrils that melt by their sweetness
  The thoughts of the parted;
And there lies, sore-sighing for thee,
  Thy love, altered-hearted.

To him the moon's icy-chill silver
  Is a sun at midday;
The fever he burns with is deeper
  Than starlight can stay:
Like one who falls stricken by arrows,
  With the colour departed
From all but his red wounds, so lies
  Thy love, bleeding-hearted.

To the music the banded bees make him
  He closeth his ear;
In the blossoms their small horns are blowing
  The honey-song clear;
But as if every sting to his bosom
  Its smart had imparted,
Low lies by the edge of the river,
  Thy love, aching-hearted.

By the edge of the river, far wandered
  From his once beloved bowers,
And the haunts of his beautiful playmates,
  And the beds strewn with flowers;
Now thy name is his playmate—that only!—
  And the hard rocks upstarted
From the sand make the couch where he lies,
  Thy Krishna, sad-hearted.

Oh may Hari fill each soul,
As these gentle verses roll
Telling of the anguish borne
By kindred ones asunder torn!
Oh may Hari unto each
All the lore of loving teach,
All the pain and all the bliss:
Jayadeva prayeth this!

Yea, Lady! in the self-same spot he waits
Where with thy kiss thou taught'st him utmost love,
And drew him, as none else draws, with thy look;
And all day long, and all night long, his cry

Is "Radha, Radha," like a spell said o'er;
And in his heart there lives no wish nor hope
Save only this, to slake his spirit's thirst
For Radha's love on Radha's lips; and find
Peace in the immortal beauty of thy brow.

(*What follows is to the Music* GURJJARÎ *and the Mode* EKATÂLÎ.)

Mistress, sweet and bright and holy!
  Meet him in that place;
Change his cheerless melancholy
  Into joy and grace;
If thou hast forgiven, vex not;
  If thou lovest, go;
Watching ever by the river,
  Krishna listens low:

Listens low, and on his reed there
  Softly sounds thy name,
Making even mute things plead there
  For his hope: 'tis shame

That, while winds are welcome to him,
  If from thee they blow,
Mournful ever by the river
  Krishna waits thee so!

When a bird's wing stirs the roses,
  When a leaf falls dead,
Twenty times he recomposes
  The flower-seat he has spread:
Twenty times, with anxious glances
  Seeking thee in vain,
Sighing ever by the river,
  Krishna droops again.

Loosen from thy foot the bangle,
  Lest its golden bell,
With a tiny, tattling jangle,
  Any false tale tell:
If thou fearest that the moonlight
  Will thy glad face know,
Draw those dark braids lower, Lady!
  But to Krishna go.

Swift and still as lightning's splendour
  Let thy beauty come,
Sudden, gracious, dazzling, tender,
  To his arms—its home:
Swift as Indra's yellow lightning,
  Shining through the night,
Glide to Krishna's lonely bosom,
  Take him love and light.

Grant at last love's utmost measure,
  Giving, give the whole;
Keep back nothing of the treasure
  Of thy priceless soul:
Hold with both hands out unto him
  Thy chalice, let him drain
The nectar of its dearest draught,
  Till not a wish remain.

Only go—the stars are setting,
  And thy Krishna grieves;
Doubt and anger quite forgetting,
  Hasten through the leaves:

Wherefore didst thou lead him heav'nward
But for this thing's sake?
Comfort him with pity, Radha!
Or his heart must break.

But while Jayadeva writes
This rare tale of deep delights—
Jayadev, whose heart is given
Unto Hari, Lord in Heaven—
See that ye too, as ye read,
With a glad and humble heed,
Bend your brows before His face,
That ye may have bliss and grace.

And then the Maid, compassionate, sang on—

Lady, most sweet!
For thy coming feet
He listens in the wood, with love sore-tried;
Faintly sighing,
Like one a-dying,
He sends his thoughts afoot to meet his bride.

Ah, silent one!
Sunk is the sun,
The darkness falls as deep as Krishna's sorrow;
The chakor's strain
Is not more vain
Than mine, and soon grey dawn will bring white
morrow.

And thine own bliss
Delays by this;
The utmost of thy heaven comes only so
When, with hearts beating
And passionate greeting,
Parting is over, and the parted grow

One—one for ever!
And the old endeavour
To be so blended is assuaged at last;
And the glad tears raining
Have nought remaining
Of doubt or 'plaining; and the dread has passed

Out of each face,
In the close embrace,
That by-and-by embracing will be over;
The ache that causes
Those mournful pauses
In bowers of earth between lover and lover:

To be no more felt,
To fade, to melt
In the strong certainty of joys immortal;
In the glad meeting,
And quick sweet greeting
Of lips that close beyond Time's shadowy portal.

And to thee is given,
Angel of Heaven!
This glory and this joy with Krishna. Go!
Let him attain,
For his loug pain,
The prize it promised,—see thee coming slow

A vision first, but then—
By glade and glen—
A lovely, loving soul, true to its home;
His Queen—his Crown—his All,
Hast'ning at last to fall
Upon his breast, and live there. Radha, come!

Come! and come thou, Lord of all;
Unto whom the Three Worlds call:
Thou, that didst in angry might,
Kansa, like a comet, smite;
Thou, that in thy passion tender,
An incarnate spell and splendour,
Hung on Radha's glorious face—
In the garb of Krishna's grace—
As above the bloom the bee,
When the honeyed revelry
Is too subtle-sweet an one
Not to hang and dally on.
Thou that art the Three Worlds' glory
Of life the light, of every story

The meaning and the mark, of love
The root and flower, o' the sky above
The blue, of bliss the heart, of those
The lovers, that which did impose
The gentle law, that each should be
The other's Heav'n and harmony.

(Here ends that Sarga of the Gita Govinda entitled

ṢAKANDKSHAPUNDARIKAKSHO.)

SARGA THE SIXTH.

DHRISHTAVAIKUNTO.

KRISHNA MADE BOLDER.

BUT seeing that, for all her loving will,
The flower-soft feet of Radha had not power
To leave their place and go, she sped again—
That maiden—and to Krishna's eager ears
Told how it fared with his sweet mistress there.

(*What follows is to the Music* GONDAKIRÎ *and the Mode* RUPAKA.)

Krishna! 'tis thou must come, (she sang)
  Ever she waits thee in heavenly bower;
The lotus seeks not the wandering bee,
  The bee must find the flower.

All the wood over her deep eyes roam,
  Marvelling sore where tarries the bee,
Who leaves such lips of nectar unsought
  As those that blossom for thee.

Her steps would fail if she tried to come,
  Would falter and fail, with yearning weak;
At the first of the road they would falter and pause,
  And the way is strange to seek.

Find her where she is sitting, then,
  With lotus-blossom on ankle and arm
Wearing thine emblems, and musing of nought
  But the meeting to be—glad, warm.

To be—"but wherefore tarrieth he?"
  "What can stay or delay him?—go!
See if the soul of Krishna comes,"
  Ten times she sayeth to me so;

  Ten times lost in a languorous swoon,
    "Now he cometh—he cometh," she cries;

And a love-look lights her eyes in the gloom,
  And the darkness is sweet with her sighs.

Till, watching in vain, she sinks again
  Under the shade of the whispering leaves,
With a heart too full of its love at last
  To heed how her bosom heaves.

Shall not these fair verses swell
The number of the wise who dwell
In the realm of Kama's bliss?
Jayadeva prayeth this,
Jayadev, the bard of Love,
Servant of the Gods above.

For all so strong in Heaven itself
  Is Love, that Radha sits drooping there,
Her beautiful bosoms panting with thought,
  And the braids drawn back from her ear.

And—angel albeit—her rich lips breathe
  Sighs, if sighs were ever so sweet;

And—if spirits can tremble—she trembles now
  From forehead to jewelled feet.

And her voice of music sinks to a sob,
  And her eyes, like eyes of a mated roe,
Are tender with looks of yielded love,
  With dreams dreamed long ago;

Long—long ago, but soon to grow real,
  To end, and be waking and certain and true;
Of which dear surety murmur her lips,
  As the lips of sleepers do:

And, dreaming, she loosens her girdle-pearls,
  And opens her arms to the empty air,
Then starts if a leaf of the champâk falls,
  Sighing, "O leaf! is he there?"

Why dost thou linger in this dull spot,
  Haunted by serpents and evil for thee?
Why not hasten to Nanda's House?
  It is plain, if thine eyes could see.

May these words of high-endeavour—
Full of grace and gentle favour—
Find out those whose hearts can feel
What the message did reveal,
Words that Radha's messenger
Unto Krishna took from her,
Slowly guiding him to come
Through the forest to his home,
Guiding him to find the road
Which led—though long—to Love's abode.

(*Here ends that Sarga of the Gîta Govinda entitled*
DHRISHTAVAIKUNTO.)

SARGA THE SEVENTH.

VIPRALABDHAVARNANE NAGARANARAYANO.

KRISHNA SUPPOSED FALSE.

MEANTIME the moon, the rolling moon, clomb high,
And over all Vrindávana it shone;
The moon which on the front of gentle night
Gleams like the chundun-mark on beauty's brow;
The conscious moon which hath its silver face
Marred with the shame of lighting earthly loves:

And while the round white lamp of earth rose higher,
And still he tarried, Radha, petulant,
Sang soft impatience and half-earnest fears.

(*What follows is to the Music* MÂLAVA *and the Mode* YATI.)

'Tis time!—he comes not!—will he come?
  Can he leave me thus to pine?
Yami hê kam sharanam!
  Ah! what refuge then is mine?

For his sake I sought the wood,
  Threaded dark and devious ways;
Yami hê kam sharanam!
  Can it be Krishna betrays?

Let me die then, and forget
  Anguish, patience, hope, and fear;
Yami hê kam sharanam!
  Ah, why have I held him dear?

Ah, this soft night torments me,
  Thinking that his faithless arms—
Yami hê kam sharanam!—
  Clasp some shadow of my charms.

Fatal shadow—foolish mock!
  When the great love shone confessed;—
Yami hê kam sharanam!
  Krishna's lotus loads my breast;

'Tis too heavy, lacking him;
  Like a broken flower I am—
Necklets, jewels, what are ye?
  Yami hê kam sharanam!

Yami hê kam sharanam!
  The sky is still, the forest sleeps;
Krishna forgets—he loves no more;
  He fails in faith, and Radha weeps.

But the poet Jayadev—
He who is great Hari's slave,
He who finds asylum sweet
Only at great Hari's feet;
He who for your comfort sings
All this to the Vina's strings—

Prays that Radha's tender moan
In your hearts be thought upon,
And that all her holy grace
Live there like the loved one's face.

Yet, if I wrong him (sang she)—can he fail ?
Could any in the wood win back his kisses ?
Could any softest lips of earth prevail
To hold him from my arms ? any love-blisses

Blind him once more to mine ? O Soul, my prize !
Art thou not merely hindered at this hour ?
Sore-wearied, wandering, lost ? how otherwise
Shouldst thou not hasten to the bridal-bower ?

But seeing far away that Maiden come
Alone, with eyes cast down and lingering steps,
Again a little while she feared to hear
Of Krishna false ; and her quick thoughts took shape
In a fine jealousy, with words like these—

Something then of earth has held him
  From his home above,
Some one of those slight deceivers—
  Ah, my foolish love!

Some new face, some winsome playmate,
  With her hair untied,
And the blossoms tangled in it,
  Woos him to her side.

On the dark orbs of her bosom—
  Passionately heaved—
Sink and rise the warm, white pearl-strings,
  Oh, my love deceived!

Fair? yes, yes! the rippled shadow
  Of that midnight hair
Shows above her brow—as clouds do
  O'er the moon—most fair:

And she knows, with wilful paces,
  How to make her zone
Gleam and please him; and her ear-rings
  Tinkle love; and grown

Coy as he grows fond, she meets him
  With a modest show;
Shaming truth with truthful seeming,
  While her laugh—light, low—

And her subtle mouth that murmurs,
  And her silken cheek,
And her eyes, say she dissembles
  Plain as speech could speak.

Till at length, a fatal victress,
  Of her triumph vain,
On his neck she lies and smiles there :—
  Ah, my Joy!—my Pain!

But may Radha's fond annoy,
And may Krishna's dawning joy,
Warm and waken love more fit—
Jayadeva prayeth it—
And the griefs and sins assuage
Of this blind and evil age.

O Moon! (she sang) that art so pure and pale,
  Is Krishna wan like thee with lonely waiting?
O lamp of love! art thou the lover's friend,
  And wilt not bring him, my long pain abating?
O fruitless moon! thou dost increase my pain;
O faithless Krishna! I have striven in vain.

And then, lost in her fancies sad, she moaned—

(*What follows is to the Music* GURJJARÎ *and the Mode* EKATÂLÎ.)

In vain, in vain!
Earth will of earth! I mourn more than I blame;
  If he had known, he would not sit and paint
The tilka on her smooth black brow, nor claim
  Quick kisses from her yielded lips—false, faint—
False, fragrant, fatal! Krishna's quest is o'er
By Jumna's shore!

Vain—it was vain!
The temptress was too near, the heav'n too far;

I can but weep because he sits and ties
Garlands of fire-flowers for her loosened hair,
And in its silken shadow veils his eyes
And buries his fond face. Yet I forgave
By Jumna's wave!

Vainly! all vain!
Make then the most of that whereto thou'rt given,
Feign her thy Paradise—thy Love of loves;
Say that her eyes are stars, her face the heaven,
Her bosoms the two worlds, with sandal-groves
Faint-scented, and the kiss-marks—ah, thy dream
By Jumna's stream!

It shall be vain!
And vain to string the emeralds on her arm
And hang the milky pearls upon her neck,
Saying they are not jewels, but a swarm
Of crowded, glossy bees, come there to suck
The rosebuds of her breast, the sweetest flowers
Of Jumna's bowers.

That shall be vain!
Nor wilt thou so believe thine own blind wooing,
Nor slake thy heart's thirst even with the cup
Which at the last she brims for thee, undoing
Her girdle of carved gold, and yielding up,
Love's uttermost: brief the poor gain and pride
By Jumna's tide.

Because still vain
Is love that feeds on shadow; vain, as thou dost,
To look so deep into the phantom eyes
For that which lives not there; and vain, as thou must,
To marvel why the painted pleasure flies,
When the fair, false wings seemed folded for ever
By Jumna's river.

And vain! yes, vain!
For me too is it, having so much striven,
To see this fine snare take thee, and thy soul
Which should have climbed to mine, and shared my heaven,
Spent on a lower loveliness, whose whole

Passion of love were but a parody
Of that kept here for thee.

Ahaha! vain!
For on some isle of Jumna's silver stream
He gives all that they ask to those dull eyes,
While mine which are his angel's, mine which gleam
With light that might have led him to the skies—
That almost led him—are eclipsed with tears
Wailing my fruitless prayers.

But thou, good Friend,
Hang not thy head for shame, nor come so slowly,
As one whose message is too hard to tell;
If thou must say Krishna is forfeit wholly—
Wholly forsworn and lost—let the grief dwell
Where the sin doth,—except in this sad heart,
Which cannot shun its part.

O great Hari! purge from wrong
The soul of him who writes this song;
Purge the souls of those that read
From every fault of thought and deed;

With thy blessed light assuage
The darkness of this evil age!
Jayadev the bard of love,
Servant of the Gods above,
Prays it for himself and you—
Gentle hearts who listen!—too.

Then in this other strain she wailed his loss—

(*What follows is to the Music* DESHAVARÂDÎ *and the Mode* RUPAKA.)

She, not Radha, wins the crown
Whose false lips were dearest;
What was distant gain to him
When sweet loss seemed nearest?
Love her, therefore, lulled to loss
On her fatal bosom;
Love her with such love as she
Can give back in the blossom.

Love her, O thou rash lost soul!
With thy thousand graces;
Coin rare thoughts into fair words
For her face of faces;

Praise it, fling away for it
 Life's purpose in a sigh,
All for those lips like flower-leaves,
 And lotus-dark deep eye.

Nay, and thou shalt be happy too
 Till the fond dream is over;
And she shall taste delight to hear
 The wooing of her lover;
The breeze that brings the sandal up
 From distant green Malay,
Shall seem all fragrance in the night,
 All coolness in the day.

The crescent moon shall seem to swim
 Only that she may see
The glad eyes of my Krishna gleam,
 And her soft glances he:
It shall be as a silver lamp
 Set in the sky to show
The rose-leaf palms that cling and clasp,
 And the breast that beats below.

The thought of parting shall not lie
  Cold on their throbbing lives,
The dread of ending shall not chill
  The glow beginning gives;
She in her beauty dark shall look—
  As long as clouds can be—
As gracious as the rain-time cloud
  Kissing the shining sea.

And he, amid his playmates old,
  At least a little while,
Shall not breathe forth again the sigh
  That spoils the song and smile;
Shall be left wholly to his choice,
  Free for his pleasant sin,
With the golden-girdled damsels
  Of the bowers I found him in.

For me, his Angel, only
  The sorrow and the smart,
The pale grief sitting on the brow
  The dead hope in the heart;

For me the loss of losing,
For me the ache and dearth;
My king crowned with the wood-flowers!
My fairest upon earth!

Hari, Lord and King of love!
From thy throne of light above
Stoop to help us, deign to take
Our spirits to thee for the sake
Of this song, which speaks the fears
Of all who weep with Radha's tears.

But love is strong to pardon, slow to part,
And still the Lady, in her fancies, sang—

Wind of the Indian stream!
A little—oh! a little—breathe once more
The fragrance like his mouth's! blow from thy shore
A last word as he fades into a dream;

Bodiless Lord of love!
Show him once more to me a minute's space,
My Krishna, with the love-look in his face,
And then I come to my own place above;

I will depart and give
All back to Fate and her: I will submit
To thy stern will, and bow myself to it,
Enduring still, though desolate, to live;

If it indeed be life,
Even so resigning, to sit patience-mad,
To feel the zephyrs burn, the sunlight sad,
The peace of holy heaven, a restless strife.

Haho! what words are these?
How can I live and lose him? how not go
Whither love draws me for a soul loved so?
How yet endure such sorrow?—or how cease?

Wind of the Indian wave!
If that thou canst, blow poison here, not nard;
God of the five shafts! shoot thy sharpest hard,
And kill me, Radha,—Radha who forgave!

Or, bitter River,
Yamûn! be Yama's sister! be Death's kin!
Swell thy wave up to me and gulf me in,
Cooling this cruel, burning pain for ever.

Ah! if only visions stir
Grief so passionate in her.
What divine grief will not take.
Spirits in heaven for the sake
Of those who miss love? Oh, be wise!
Mark this story of the skies,
Meditate Govinda ever,
Sitting by the sacred river,
The mystic stream which o'er his feet
Glides slow, with murmurs low and sweet,
Till none can tell whether those be
Blue lotus-blooms, seen veiledly
Under the wave, or mirrored gems
Reflected from the diadems
Bound on the brows of mighty Gods,
Who lean from out their pure abodes,
And leave their bright felicities
To guide great Krishna to his skies.

(*Here ends that Sarga of the Gîta Govinda entitled* VIPRALABDHAVARNANE NAGARANARAYANO.)

SARGA THE EIGHTH.

KHANDITAVARNANE VILAKSHALAKSHMIPATI.

THE REBUKING OF KRISHNA.

FOR when the weary night had worn away
In these vain fears, and the clear morning broke,
Lo, Krishna! lo, the longed-for of her soul
Came too!—in the glad light he came and bent
His knees and clasped his hands; on his dumb lips
Fear, wonder, joy, passion, and reverence
Strove for the trembling words, and Radha knew
Joy won for him and her; yet none the less
A little time she chided him, and sang,

(*What follows is to the Music* Bhairavî *and the Mode* Yati.)

Krishna!—then thou hast found me!—and thine eyes
  Heavy and sad and stained as if with weeping!
Ah! is it not that those which were thy prize
  So radiant seemed that all night thou wert keeping
Vigils of tender wooing?—have thy Love!
  Here is no place for vows broken in making;
Thou Lotus-eyed! thou soul for whom I strove!
  Go! ere I listen, my just mind forsaking.

Krishna! my Krishna with the woodland-wreath!
  Return, or I shall soften as I blame;
The while thy very lips are dark to the teeth
  With dye that from her lids and lashes came,
Left on the mouth I touched. Fair traitor! go!
  Say not they darkened, lacking food and sleep
Long waiting for my face; I turn it—so—
  Go! ere I half believe thee, pleading deep;

But wilt thou plead, when, like a love-verse printed
  On the smooth polish of an emerald,
I see the marks she stamped, the kisses dinted
  Large-lettered, by her lips? thy speech withheld
Speaks all too plainly; go,—abide thy choice!
  If thou dost stay, I shall more greatly grieve thee;
Not records of her victory?—peace, dear voice!
  Hence with that godlike brow, lest I believe thee.

For dar'st thou feign the saffron on thy bosom
  Was not implanted in disloyal embrace?
Or that this many-coloured love-tree blossom
  Shone not, but yesternight, above her face?
Comest thou here, so late, to be forgiven
  O thou, in whose eyes Truth was made to live?
O thou, so worthy else of grace and heaven?
  O thou, so nearly won? Ere I forgive,

Go, Krishna! go!—lest I should think, uuwise,
  Thy heart not false, as thy long lingering seems,
Lest, seeing myself so imaged in thine eyes,
  I shame the name of Pity—turn to dreams

The sacred sound of vows; make Virtue grudge
  Her praise to Mercy, calling thy sin slight;
Go therefore, dear offender! go! thy Judge
  Had best not see thee to give sentence right.*

But may he grant us peace at last and bliss
Who heard and smiled to hear delays like this,
Delays that dallied with a dream come true,
Fond wilful angers; for the maid smiled too
To see, as Radha ended, her hand take
His dark robe for her veil, and Krishna make
The word she spoke for parting kindliest sign
He should not go, but stay. O grace divine,
Be ours too! Jayadev, the Poet of love,
Prays it from Hari, lordliest above.

(*Here ends that Sarga of the Gîta Govinda entitled*
KHANDITAVARNANE VILAKSHALAKSHMIPATI.)

---

* The text here is not closely followed.

SARGA THE NINTH.

KALAHANTARITAVARNANE MUGDHAMUKUNDO.

THE END OF KRISHNA'S TRIAL.

YET not quite did the doubts of Radha die,
Nor her sweet brows unbend; but she, the Maid—
Knowing her heart so tender, her soft arms
Aching to take him in, her rich mouth sad
For the comfort of his kiss, and these fears false—
Spake yet a little in fair words like these,

(*What follows is to the Music* GURJJARÎ *and the Mode* YATI.)

The lesson that thy faithful love has taught him
He has heard;
The wind of spring obeying thee hath brought him
At thy word;

What joy in all the three worlds was so precious
To thy mind?
Mâ kooroo mânini mânamayè,*
Ah, be kind!

No longer from his earnest eyes conceal
Thy delights;
Lift thy face, and let the jealous veil reveal
All his rights;
The glory of thy beauty was but given
For content;
Mâ kooroo mânini mânamayè,
Oh, relent!

Remember, being distant, how he bore thee
In his heart;
Look on him sadly turning from before thee
To depart;
Is he not the soul thou lovedst, sitting lonely
In the wood?
Mâ kooroo mânini mânamayè,
'Tis not good!

---

* My proud one! do not indulge in scorn.

He who grants thee high delight in bridal-bower
Pardons long;
What the gods do love may do at such an hour
Without wrong;
Why weepest thou? why keepest thou in anger
Thy lashes down?
Mâ kooroo mânini mânamayè
Do not frown!

Lift thine eyes now, and look on him, bestowing,
Without speech;
Let him pluck at last the flower so sweetly growing
In his reach;
The fruit of lips, of loving tones, of glances
That forgive;
Mâ kooroo mânini mânamayè
Let him live!

Let him speak with thee, and pray to thee, and prove thee
All his truth;
Let his silent loving lamentation move thee
Asking ruth;

How knowest thou? Ah, listen, dearest Lady,
He is there;
Mâ kooroo mânini mânamayè
Thou must hear!

O rare voice, which is a spell
Unto all on earth who dwell!
O rich voice of rapturous love,
Making melody above!
Krishna's, Hari's—one in two,
Sound these mortal verses through!
Sound like that soft flute which made
Such a magic in the shade—
Calling deer-eyed maidens nigh,
Waking wish and stirring sigh,
Whirling heads and melting breasts,
Whispering love's divine unrests,
Winning blessings to descend,
Bringing earthly ills to end;—
Be thou heard in this song now
Thou, the great Enchantment, thou!

(*Here ends that Sarga of the Gîta Govinda entitled*
KALAHANTARITAVARNANE MUGDHAMUKUNDO.)

SARGA THE TENTH.

MANINIVARNANE CHATURACHATURBHUJO.

KRISHNA IN PARADISE.

BUT she, abasing still her glorious eyes,
And still not yielding all her face to him,
Relented, till with softer upturned look
She smiled while the Maid pleaded ; so thereat
Came Krishna nearer, and his eager lips
Mixed sighs with words in this fond song he sang,

(*What follows is to the Music* DESHÎYAVARÂDÎ *and the Mode* ASHTATÂLÎ.)

O angel of my hope ! O my heart's home !
  My fear is lost in love, my love in fear ;
This bids me trust my burning wish, and come,
  That checks me with its memories, drawing near :

Lift up thy look, and let the thing it saith
End fear with grace, or darken love to death.

Or only speak once more, for though thou slay me,
  Thy heavenly mouth must move, and I shall hear
Dulcet delights of perfect music sway me
  Again—again that voice so blest and dear;
Sweet Judge! the prisoner prayeth for his doom
That he may hear his fate divinely come.

Speak once more! then thou canst not choose but show
  Thy mouth's unparalleled and honeyed wonder
Where, like pearls hid in red-lipped shells, the row
  Of pearly teeth thy rose-red lips lie under;
Ah me! I am that bird that woos the moon,
And pipes—poor fool! to make it glitter soon.

Yet hear me on—because I cannot stay
  The passion of my soul, because my gladness
Will pour forth from my heart,—from that far day
  When through the mist of all my sin and sadness

Thou didst vouchsafe—Surpassing One!—to break,
All else I slighted for thy noblest sake.

Thou, thou hast been my blood, my breath, my being;
  The pearl to plunge for in the sea of life;
The sight to strain for, past the bounds of seeing;
  The victory to win through longest strife;
My Queen! my crownèd Mistress! my sphered bride!
Take this for truth, that what I say beside

Of bold love—grown full-orbed at sight of thee—
  May be forgiven with a quick remission;
For, thou divine fulfilment of all hope,
  Thou all-undreamed completion of the vision!
I gaze upon thy beauty, and my fear
Passes as clouds do, when the moon shines clear.

So if thou'rt angry still, this shall avail,
  Look straight at me, and let thy bright glance wound
    me;
Fetter me! gyve me! lock me in the gaol
  Of thy delicious arms; make fast around me

The silk-soft manacles of wrists and hands,
Then kill me! I shall never break those bands.

The starlight jewels flashing on thy breast
  Have not my right to hear thy beating heart;
The happy flower-buds that clasp thy waist
  Are soft usurpers of my place and part;
If that fair girdle only there must shine,
Give me the girdle's life—the girdle mine!

Thy brow like smooth Bandhûka-leaves; thy cheek
  Which the dark-tinted Madhuk's velvet shows;
Thy long-lashed Lotus eyes, lustrous and meek;
  Thy nose a Tila-bud; thy teeth like rows
Of Kunda-petals! he who pierceth hearts
Points with thy lovelinesses all five darts.

But Radiant, Perfect, Sweet, Supreme, forgive!
  My heart is wise—my tongue is foolish still:
I know where I am come—I know I live—
  I know that thou art Radha—that this will

Last and be heaven: that I have leave to rise
Up from thy feet, and look into thine eyes!

And, nearer coming, I ask for grace
Now that the blest eyes turn to mine;
Faithful I stand in this sacred place
Since first I saw them shine:
Dearest glory that stills my voice,
Beauty unseen, unknown, unthought!
Splendour of love, in whose sweet light
Darkness is past and nought;
Ah, beyond words that sound on earth
Golden bloom of the garden of heaven!
Radha, enchantress! Radha, the queen!
Be this trespass forgiven—
In that I dare, with courage too much
And a heart afraid,—so bold it is grown—
To hold thy hand with a bridegroom's touch,
And take thee for mine, mine own.*

---

* Much here also is necessarily paraphrased.

So they met and so they ended
Pain and parting, being blended
Life with life—made one for ever
In high love; and Jayadeva
Hasteneth on to close the story
Of their bridal grace and glory.

(*Here ends that Sarga of the Gîta Govinda entitled*
MANINIVARNANE CHATURACHATURBHUJO.)

SARGA THE ELEVENTH.

RADHIKAMILANE SANANDADAMODARO.

THE UNION OF RADHA AND KRISHNA.

THUS followed soft and lasting peace, and griefs
Died while she listened to his tender tongue,
Her eyes of antelope alight with love;
And while he led the way to the bride-bower
The maidens of her train adorned her fair
With golden marriage-cloths, and sang this song,

(*What follows is to the Music* VASANTA *and the Mode* YATI.)

Follow, happy Radha! follow,—
In the quiet falling twilight—
The steps of him who followed thee
So steadfastly and far;

Let us bring thee where the Banjulas
  Have spread a roof of crimson,
Lit up by many a marriage-lamp
  Of planet, sun, and star:
For the hours of doubt are over,
  And thy glad and faithful lover
Hath found the road by tears and prayers
  To thy divinest side;
And thou wilt not now deny him
  One delight of all thy beauty,
But yield up open-hearted
  His desire, his prize, his bride.

Oh, follow! while we fill the air
  With songs and softest music;
Lauding thy wedded loveliness,
  Dear Mistress past compare!
For there is not any splendour
  Of Apsarasas immortal—
No glory of their beauty rich—
  But Radha has a share;

Oh, follow! while we sing the song
  That fills the worlds with longing,
The music of the Lord of love
  Who melts all hearts with bliss;
For now is born the gladness
  That springs from mortal sadness,
And all soft thoughts and things and hopes
  Were presages of this.

Then, follow, happiest Lady!
  Follow him thou lovest wholly;
The hour is come to follow now
  The soul thy spells have led;
His are thy breasts like jasper-cups,
  And his thine eyes like planets;
Thy fragrant hair, thy stately neck,
  Thy queenly sumptuous head;
Thy soft small feet, thy perfect lips,
  Thy teeth like jasmine petals,
Thy gleaming rounded shoulders,
  And long caressing arms,

Being thine to give, are his; and his
  The twin strings of thy girdle,
And his the priceless treasure
  Of thine utter-sweetest charms.

So follow! while the flowers break forth
  In white and amber clusters,
At the breath of thy pure presence,
  And the radiance on thy brow;
Oh, follow where the Asokas wave
  Their sprays of gold and purple,
As if to beckon thee the way
  That Krishna passed but now;
He is gone a little forward!
  Though thy steps are faint for pleasure,
Let him hear the tattling ripple
  Of the bangles round thy feet;
Moving slowly o'er the blossoms
  On the path which he has shown thee,
That when he turns to listen
  It may make his fond heart beat.

And loose thy jewelled girdle
  A little, that its rubies
May tinkle softest music too,
  And whisper thou art near;
Though now, if in the forest
  Thou should'st bend one blade of Kusha
With silken touch of passing foot,
  His heart would know and hear;
Would hear the wood-buds saying,
  "It is Radha's foot that passes;"
Would hear the wind sigh love-sick,
  "It is Radha's fragrance, this;"
Would hear thine own heart beating
  Within thy panting bosom,
And know thee coming, coming,
  His—ever,—ever—his!

"*Mine!*"—hark! we are near enough for hearing—
  "*Soon she will come—she will smile—she will say*
Honey-sweet words of heavenly endearing;
  O soul! listen; my Bride is on her way!"

Hear'st him not, my Radha?
  Lo, night bendeth o'er thee—
Darker than dark Tamâla-leaves—
  To list thy marriage-song;
Dark as the touchstone that tries gold,
  And see now—on before thee—
Those lines of tender light that creep
  The clouded sky along:
O night! that trieth gold of love,
  This love is proven perfect!
O lines that streak the touchstone sky,
  Flash forth true shining gold!
O rose-leaf feet, go boldly!
  O night!—that lovest lovers—
Thy softest robe of silence
  About these bridals fold!

See'st thou not, my Radha?
  Lo, the night, thy bridesmaid,
Comes!—her eyes thick-painted
  With soorma of the gloom—

The night that binds the planet-worlds
  For jewels on her forehead,
And for emblem and for garland
  Loves the blue-black lotus-bloom;
The night that scents her breath so sweet
  With cool and musky odours,
That joys to spread her veil of shade
  Over the limbs of love;
And when, with loving weary,
  Yet dreaming love, they slumber,
Sets the far stars for silver lamps
  To light them from above.

So came she where he stood, awaiting her
At the bower's entry, like a god to see,
With marriage-gladness and the grace of heaven.
The great pearl set upon his glorious head
Shone like a moon among the leaves, and shone
Like stars the gems that kept her gold gown close:
But still a little while she paused—abashed
At her delight, of her deep joy afraid—
And they that tended her sang once more this,

(*What follows is to the Music* VARÂDI *and the Mode* RUPAKA.)

Enter, thrice-happy! enter, thrice-desired!
And let the gates of Hari shut thee in
With the soul destined to thee from of old.

Tremble not! lay thy lovely shame aside;
Lay it aside with thine unfastened zone,
And love him with the love that knows not fear;

Because it fears not change; enter thou in,
Flower of all sweet and stainless womanhood!
For ever to grow bright, for ever new;

Enter beneath the flowers, O flower-fair!
Beneath these tendrils, Loveliest! that entwine
And clasp, and wreathe and cling, with kissing stems;

Enter, with tender-blowing airs of heaven
Soft as love's breath and gentle as the tones
Of lover's whispers, when the lips come close:

Enter the house of Love, O loveliest!
Enter the marriage-bower, most beautiful!
And take and give the joy that Hari grants.

Thy heart has entered, let thy feet go too!
Lo, Krishna! lo, the one that thirsts for thee!
Give him the drink of amrit from thy lips.

Then she, no more delaying, entered straight;
Her step a little faltered, but her face
Shone with unutterable quick love; and—while
The music of her bangles passed the porch—
Shame, which had lingered in her downcast eyes,
Departed shamed* . . . and like the mighty deep,
Which sees the moon and rises, all his life
Uprose to drink her beams.

(*Here ends that Sarga of the Gîta Govinda entitled* RADHIKAMILANE SANANDADAMODARO.)

Hari keep you! He whose might,
On the King of Serpents seated,

---

* This complete anticipation (*salajjâ lajjâpi*) of the line—

"Upon whose brow shame is ashamed to sit"

—occurs at the close of the Sarga, part of which is here perforce omitted, along with the whole of the last one.

Flashes forth in dazzling light
  From the Great Snake's gems repeated:
Hari keep you! He whose graces,
  Manifold in majesty,—
Multiplied in heavenly places—
  Multiply on earth—to see.
Better with a hundred eyes
  Her bright charms who by him lies.

What skill may be in singing,
  What worship sound in song,
What lore be taught in loving,
  What right divined from wrong:
Such things hath Jayadeva—
  In this his Hymn of Love,
Which lauds Govinda ever,—
  Displayed; may all approve!

THE END OF THE INDIAN SONG OF SONGS.

THE RAJPOOT WIFE.

SING something, Jymul Rao! for the goats are gathered now,
And no more water is to bring;
The village-gates are set, and the night is grey as yet,
God hath given wondrous fancies to thee:—sing!

Then Jymul's supple fingers, with a touch that doubts and lingers,
Sets athrill the saddest wire of all the six;
And the girls sit in a tangle, and hush the tinkling bangle,
While the boys pile the flame with store of sticks.

And vain of village praise, but full of ancient days,
He begins with a smile and with a sigh—
"Who knows the babul-tree by the bend of the Ravee?
Quoth Gunesh, "I!" and twenty voices, "I!"

"Well—listen! there below, in the shade of bloom and
bough,
Is a musjid of carved and coloured stone;
And Abdool Shureef Khan—I spit, to name that man!—
Lieth there, underneath, all alone.

"He was Sultan Mahmood's vassal, and wore an Amir's
tassel
In his green hadj-turban, at Kurnul.
Yet the head which went so proud, it is not in his shroud;
There are bones in that grave,—but not a skull!

"And deep drove in his breast there moulders with the
rest
A dagger, brighter once than Chundra's ray;
A Rajpoot lohar whet it, and a Rajpoot woman set it
Past the power of any hand to tear away.

"'Twas the Rance Neila true, the wife of Soorj Dehu,
Lord of the Rajpoots of Nourpoor;
You shall hear the mournful story, with its sorrow and
its glory,
And curse Shureef Khan,—the soor!"

All in the wide Five-Waters was none like Soorj Dehu,
To foeman who so dreadful, to friend what heart so true?

Like Indus, through the mountains came down the
Muslim ranks,
And town-walls fell before them as flooded river-banks;

But Soorj Dehu the Rajpoot owned neither town nor
wall;
His house the camp, his roof-tree the sky that covers
all;

His seat of state the saddle; his robe a shirt of mail;
His court a thousand Rajpoots close at his stallion's tail.

Not less was Soorj a Rajah because no crown he wore
Save the grim helm of iron with sword-marks dinted o'er;

Because he grasped no sceptre save the sharp tulwar,
made
Of steel that fell from heaven,—for 'twas Indra forged
that blade!

And many a starless midnight the shout of "Soorj Dehu"
Broke up with spear and matchlock the Muslim's "Illahu."

And many a day of battle upon the Muslim proud
Fell Soorj, as Indra's lightning falls from the silent
cloud.

Nor ever shot nor arrow, nor spear nor slinger's stone,
Could pierce the mail that Neila the Ranee buckled on:

But traitor's subtle tongue-thrust through fence of steel
can break;
And Soorj was taken sleeping, whom none had ta'en
awake.

Then at the noon, in durbar, swore fiercely Shureef
Khan
That Soorj should die in torment, or live a Mussulman.

But Soorj laughed lightly at him, and answered, "Work
your will!
The last breath of my body shall curse your Prophet
still."

With words of insult shameful, and deeds of cruel kind,
They vexed that Rajpoot's body, but never moved his
mind.

And one is come who sayeth, "Ho! Rajpoots! Soorj is bound;
Your lord is caged and baited by Shureef Khan, the hound.

"The Khan hath caught and chained him, like a beast, in iron cage,
And all the camp of Islam spends on him spite and rage;

"All day the coward Muslims spend on him rage and spite;
If ye have thought to help him, 'twere good ye go to-night."

Up sprang a hundred horsemen, flashed in each hand a sword;
In each heart burned the gladness of dying for their lord;

Up rose each Rajpoot rider, and buckled on with speed
The bridle-chain and breast-cord, and the saddle of his steed.

But unto none sad Neila gave word to mount and ride;
Only she called the brothers of Soorj unto her side,

And said, "Take order straightway to seek this camp
with me;
If love and craft can conquer, a thousand is as three.

"If love be weak to save him, Soorj dies—and ye
return,
For where a Rajpoot dieth, the Rajpoot widows burn."

Thereat the Ranee Neila unbraided from her hair
The pearls as great as Kashmir grapes Soorj gave his
wife to wear,

And all across her bosoms—like lotus-buds to see—
She wrapped the tinselled sari of a dancing Kunchenee;

And fastened on her ankles the hundred silver bells,
To whose light laugh of music the Nautch-girl darts and
dwells.

And all in dress a Nautch-girl, but all in heart a
queen,
She set her foot to stirrup with a sad and settled
mien.

Only one thing she carried no Kunchenee should bear,
The knife between her bosoms;—ho, Shureef! have a care!

Thereat, with running ditty of mingled pride and pity,
  Jymul Rao makes the six wires sigh;
And the girls with tearful eyes note the music's fall
    and rise,
  And the boys let the fire fade and die.

All day lay Soorj the Rajpoot in Shureef's iron cage,
All day the coward Muslims spent on him spite and rage.

With bitter cruel torments, and deeds of shameful kind,
They racked and broke his body, but could not shake
    his mind.

And only at the Azan, when all their worst was vain,
They left him, like dogs, slinking from a lion in his pain.

No meat nor drink they gave him through all that
    burning day,
And done to death, but scornful, at twilight-time he lay.

So when the gem of Shiva uprose, the shining moon,
Soorj spake unto his spirit, "The end is coming soon.

"I would the end might hasten, could Neila only know—
What is that Nautch-girl singing with voice so known and low?

"Singing beneath the cage-bars the song of love and fear
My Neila sang at parting!—what doth that Nautch-girl here?

"Whence comes she by the music of Neila's tender strain,
She, in that shameless tinsel?—O, Nautch-girl, sing again!"

"Ah, Soorj!"—so followed answer—"here thine own Neila stands,
Faithful in life and death alike,—look up, and take my hands:

"Speak low, lest the guard hear us;—to-night, if thou
must die,
Shureef shall have no triumph, but bear thee company."

So sang she like the Koïl that dies beside its mate;
With eye as black and fearless, and love as hot and
great.

Then the Chief laid his pale lips upon the little palm,
And sank down with a smile of love, his face all glad
and calm;

And through the cage-bars Neila felt the brave heart
stop fast,
"O Soorj!"—she cried—"I follow! have patience to
the last."

She turned and went. "Who passes?" challenged the
Mussulman;
"A Nautch-girl, I."—"What seek'st thou?"—"The
presence of the Khan;

"Ask if the high chief-captain be pleased to hear me
 sing;"
And Shureef, full of feasting, the Kunchenee bade bring.

Then all before the Muslims, aflame with lawless wine,
Entered the Ranee Neila, in grace and face divine;

And all before the Muslims, wagging their goatish chins,
The Rajpoot Princess set her to the "bee-dance" that
 begins,

"*If my love loved me, he should be a bee,*
I the yellow champak, love the honey of me."

All the wreathëd movements danced she of that dance;
Not a step she slighted, not a wanton glance;

In her unveiled bosom chased th' intruding bee,
To her waist—and lower—she! a Rajpoot, she!

Sang the melting music, swayed the languorous limb:
Shureef's drunken heart beat—Shureef's eyes waxed dim.

From his finger Shureef loosed an Ormuz pearl—
"By the Prophet," quoth he, "'tis a winsome girl!

"Take this ring; and 'prithee, come and have thy pay,
I would hear at leisure more of such a lay."

Glared his eyes on her eyes, passing o'er the plain,
Glared at the tent-purdah—never glared again!

Never opened after unto gaze or glance,
Eyes that saw a Rajpoot dance a shameful dance;

For the kiss she gave him was his first and last—
Kiss of dagger, driven to his heart, and past.

At her feet he wallowed, choked with wicked blood;
In his breast the katar quivered where it stood.

At the hilt his fingers vainly—wildly—try,
Then they stiffen feeble;—die! thou slayer, die!

From his jewelled scabbard drew she Shureef's sword,
Cut atwain the neck-boue of the Muslim lord.

Underneath the starlight, sooth, a sight of dread!
Like the Goddess Kali, comes she with the head,

Comes to where her brothers guard their murdered chief;
All the camp is silent, but the night is brief.

At his feet she flings it, flings her burden vile;
"Soorj! I keep my promise! Brothers, build the pile!"

They have built it, set it, all as Rajpoots do,
From the cage of iron taken Soorj Dehu;

In the lap of Neila, seated on the pile,
Laid his head—she radiant, like a queen the while.

Then the lamp is lighted, and the ghee is poured—
"Soorj, we burn together: O my love, my lord!"

In the flame and crackle dies her tender tongue,
Dies the Ranee truest, all true wives among.

At the morn a clamour runs from tent to tent,
Like the wild geese cackling when the night is spent.

"Shureef Khan lies headless! gone is Soorj Dehu!
And the wandering Nautch-girl, who has seen her, who?"

This but know the sentries, at the "breath of dawn"
Forth there fared two horsemen, by the first was borne

The urn of clay, the vessel that Rajpoots use to bring
The ashes of dead kinsmen to Gungas' holy spring.

KING SALADIN.

LONG years ago—so tells Boccaccio
In such Italian gentleness of speech
As finds no echo in this northern air
To counterpart its music—long ago,
When Saladin was Soldan of the East,
The kings let cry a general crusade;
And to the trysting-plains of Lombardy
The idle lances of the North and West
Rode all that spring, as all the spring runs down
Into a lake, from all its hanging hills,
The clash and glitter of a hundred streams.

Whereof the rumour reached to Saladin,
And that swart king—as royal in his heart
As any crownèd champion of the Cross—
That he might fully, of his knowledge, learn

The purpose of the lords of Christendom,
And when their war and what their armament,
Took thought to cross the seas to Lombardy.
Wherefore, with wise and trustful Amirs twain,
All habited in garbs that merchants use;
With trader's band and gipsire on the breast
That best loved mail and dagger, Saladin
Set forth upon his journey perilous.
In that day, fairest land was Lombardy!
A sea of country-plenty, islanded
With cities rich; nor richer one than thee,
Marble Milano! from whose gate at dawn—
With ear that little recked the matin-bell,
But a keen eye to measure wall and foss—
The Soldan rode; and all day long he rode
For Pavia; passing basilic, and shrine,
And gaze of vineyard-workers, wotting not
Yon trader was the Lord of Heathenesse.
All day he rode; yet at the wane of day
No gleam of gate, or ramp, or rising spire,
Nor Tessin's sparkle underneath the stars
Promised him Pavia; but he was 'ware

Of a gay company upon the way,
Ladies and lords, with horses, hawks, and hounds;
Cap-plumes and tresses fluttered by the wind
Of merry race for home. "Go!" said the king
To him that rode upon his better hand,
"And pray these gentles of their courtesy
How many leagues to Pavia, and the gates
What hour they close them?" Then the Saracen
Set spur, and being joined to one that seemed
First of the hunt, he told the message—they
Checking the jangling bits, and chiding down
The unfinished laugh to listen—but by this
Came up the king, his bonnet in his hand,
Theirs doffed to him: "Sir Trader," Torel said
(Messer Torello 'twas, of Istria),
"They shut the Pavian gate at even-song,
And even-song is sung." Then turning half,
Muttered, "Pardie, the man is worshipful,
A stranger too!" "Fair lord!" quoth Saladin,
"Please you to stead some weary travellers,
Saying where we may lodge, the town so far
And night so near." "Of my heart, willingly,"

Made answer Torel, "I did think but now
To send my knave an errand—he shall ride
And bring you unto lodgment—oh! no thanks,
Our Lady keep you!" then with whispered hest
He called their guide and sped them. Being gone,
Torello told his purpose, and the band,
With ready zeal and loosened bridle-chains,
Rode for his hunting-palace, where they set
A goodly banquet underneath the planes,
And hung the house with guest-lights, and anon
Welcomed the wondering strangers, thereto led
Unwitting, by a world of winding paths;
Messer Torello, at the inner gate,
Waiting to take them in—a goodly host,
Stamped current with God's image for a man
Chief among men, truthful, and just, and free.
Then he, "Well met again, fair sirs! Our knave
Hath found you shelter better than the worst:
Please you to leave your selles, and being bathed,
Grace our poor supper here." Then Saladin,
Whose sword had yielded ere his courtesy,

Answered, "Great thanks, Sir Knight, and this
much blame,
You spoil us for our trade! two bonnets doffed,
And travellers' questions holding you afield,
For those you give us this." "Sir! not your meed,
Nor worthy of your breeding; but in sooth
That is not out of Pavia." Therewithal
He led them to fair chambers decked with all
Makes tired men glad; lights, and the marble bath,
And flasks that sparkled, liquid amethyst,
And grapes, not dry as yet from evening dew.
Thereafter at the supper-board they sat;
Nor lacked it, though its guest was reared a king,
Worthy provend in crafts of cookery,
Pastel, pasticcio—all set forth on gold;
And gracious talk and pleasant courtesies,
Spoken in stately Latin, cheated time
Till there was none but held the stranger-sir,
For all his chapman's dress of cramasie,
Goodlier than silks could make him. Presently
Talk rose upon the Holy Sepulchre:
"I go myself," said Torel, "with a score

Of better knights—the flower of Pavia—
To try our steel against King Saladin's.
Sirs! ye have seen the countries of the Sun,
Know you the Soldan?" Answer gave the king,
"The Soldan we have seen—'twill push him hard
If, which I nothing doubt, you Pavian lords
Are valorous as gentle;—we, alas!
Are Cyprus merchants making trade to France—
Dull sons of Peace." "By Mary!" Torel cried,
"But for thy word, I ne'er heard speech so fit
To lead the war, nor saw a hand that sat
Liker a soldier's in the sabre's place;
But sure I hold you sleepless!" Then himself
Playing the chamberlain, with torches borne,
Led them to restful beds, commending them
To sleep and God, who hears—Allah or God—
When good men do his creatures charities.

At dawn the cock, and neigh of saddled steeds,
Broke the king's dreams of battle—not their own,
But goodly jennets from Torello's stalls,
Caparisoned to bear them; he their host
Up, with a gracious radiance like the sun,

To bid them speed. Beside him in the court
Stood Dame Adalieta; comely she,
And of her port as stately, and serene
As if the braided gold about her brows
Had been a crown. Mutual good-morrow given,
Thanks said and stayed, the lady prayed her guest
To take a token of his sojourn there,
Marking her good-will, not his worthiness;
"A gown of miniver—these furbelows
Are silk I spun—my lord wears ever such—
A housewife's gift! but those ye love are far;
Wear it as given for them." Then Saladin—
"A queenly gift, Madonna, past my thanks;
And—but thou shalt not hear a 'no' from me—
Past my receiving; yet I take it; we
Were debtors to your noble courtesy
Out of redemption—this but bankrupts us."
"Nay, sir,—God shield you!" said the knight and
dame.
And Saladin, with phrase of gentilesse
Returned, or ever that he rode alone,
Swore a great oath in guttural Arabic,

An oath by Allah—startling up the ears
Of those three Christian cattle they bestrode—
That never yet was nobler-natured man,
Nor gentler lady;—and that time should see
For a king's lodging quittance royal repaid.

It was the day of the Passaggio:
Ashore the war-steeds champed the burnished bit;
Afloat the galleys tugged the mooring-chain:
The town was out; the Lombard armourers—
Red-hot with riveting the helmets up,
And whetting axes for the heathen heads—
Cooled in the crowd that filled the squares and streets
To speed God's soldiers. At the none that day
Messer Torello to the gate came down,
Leading his lady;—sorrow's hueless rose
Grew on her cheek, and thrice the destrier
Struck fire, impatient, from the pavement-squares,
Or ere she spoke, tears in her lifted eyes,
"Goest thou, lord of mine?" "Madonna, yes!"

Said Torel, "for my soul's weal and the Lord
Ride I to-day: my good name and my house
Reliant I entrust thee, and—because
It may be they shall slay me, and because,
Being so young, so fair, and so reputed,
The noblest will entreat thee—wait for me,
Widow or wife, a year, and month, and day;
Then if thy kinsmen press thee to a choice,
And if I be not come, hold me for dead;
Nor link thy blooming beauty with the grave
Against thine heart." "Good my lord!" answered
she,
"Hardly my heart sustains to let thee go;
Thy memory it can keep, and keep it will,
Though my one lord, Torel of Istria,
Live, or——" "Sweet, comfort thee! San Pietro
speed!
I shall come home: if not, and worthy knees
Bend for this hand, whereof none worthy lives,
Least he who lays his last kiss thus upon it,
Look thee, I free it——" "Nay!" she said, "but I,
A petulant slave that hugs her golden chain,

Give that gift back, and with it this poor ring:
Set it upon thy sword-hand, and in fight
Be merciful and win, thinking of me."
Then she, with pretty action, drawing on
Her ruby, buckled over it his glove—
The great steel glove—and through the helmet bars
Took her last kiss;—then let the chafing steed
Have its hot will and go.

But Saladin,
Safe back among his lords at Lebanon,
Well wotting of their quest, awaited it,
And held the Crescent up against the Cross.
In many a doughty fight Ferrara blades
Clashed with keen Damasc, many a weary month
Wasted afield; but yet the Christians
Won nothing nearer to Christ's sepulchre;
Nay, but gave ground. At last, in Acre pent,
On their loose files, enfeebled by the war,
Came stronger smiter than the Saracen—
The deadly Pest: day after day they died,
Pikeman and knight-at-arms; day after day
A thinner line upon the leaguered wall

Held off the heathen :—held them off a space ;
Then, over-weakened, yielded, and gave up
The city and the stricken garrison.
  So to sad chains and hateful servitude
Fell all those purple lords—Christendom's stars,
Once high in hope as soaring Lucifer,
Now low as sinking Hesper : with them fell
Messer Torello—never one so poor
Of all the hundreds that his bounty fed
As he in prison—ill-entreated, bound,
Starved of sweet light, and set to shameful tasks ;
And that great load at heart to know the days
Fast flying, and to live accounted dead.
One joy his gaolers left him,—his good hawk ;
The brave, gay bird that crossed the seas with him :
And often, in the mindful hour of eve,
With tameless eye and spirit masterful,
In a feigned anger checking at his hand,
The good grey falcon made his master cheer.

One day it chanced Saladin rode afield
With shawled and turbaned Amirs, and his hawks—

Lebanon-bred, and mewed as princes lodge—
Flew foul, forgot their feather, hung at wrist,
And slighted call. The Soldan, quick in wrath,
Bade slay the cravens, scourge the falconer,
And seek some wight who knew the heart of hawks,
To keep it hot and true. Then spake a Sheikh—
"There is a Frank in prison by the sea,
Far-seen herein." "Give word that he be brought,"
Quoth Saladin, "and bid him set a cast:
If he hath skill, it shall go well for him."

Thus by the winding path of circumstance
One palace held, as prisoner and prince,
Torello and his guest: unwitting each,
Nay and unwitting, though they met and spake
Of that goshawk and this—signors in serge,
And chapmen crowned, who knows?—till on a time
Some trick of face, the manner of some smile,
Some gleam of sunset from the glad day gone,
Caught the king's eye, and held it. "Nazarene!
What native art thou?" asked he. "Lombard I,
A man of Pavia." "And thy name?" "Torel,

Messer Torello known in happier times,
Now best unknown." "Come hither, Christian!"
The Soldan said, and led the way, by court
And hall and fountain, to an inner room
Rich with king's robes: therefrom he reached a gown,
And "Know'st thou this?" he asked. "High lord! I might
Elsewhere," quoth Torel, "here 'twere mad to say
Yon gown my wife unto a trader gave
That shared our board." "Nay, but that gown is this,
And she the giver, and the trader I,"
Quoth Saladin; "I! twice a king to-day,
Owing a royal debt and paying it."
Then Torel, sore amazed, "Great lord, I blush,
Remembering how the Master of the East
Lodged sorrily." "It's Master's Master thou!"
Gave answer Saladin, "come in and see
What wares the Cyprus traders keep at home;
Come forth and take thy place, Saladin's friend."
Therewith into the circle of his lords,
With gracious mien the Soldan led his slave;
And while the dark eyes glittered, seated him

First of the full divan. "Orient lords,"
So spake he,—"let the one who loves his king
Honour this Frank, whose house sheltered your king;
He is my brother:" then the night-black beards
Swept the stone floor in ready reverence,
Agas and Amirs welcoming Torel:
And a great feast was set, the Soldan's friend
Royally garbed, upon the Soldan's hand,
Shining the bright star of the banqueters.

All which, and the abounding grace and love
Shown him by Saladin, a little held
The heart of Torel from its Lombard home
With Dame Adalieta: but it chanced
He sat beside the king in audience,
And there came one who said, "Oh, Lord of lords,
That galley of the Genovese which sailed
With Frankish prisoners is gone down at sea."
"Gone down!" cried Torel. "Ay! what recks it,
friend,

To fall thy visage for?" quoth Saladin;
"One galley less to ship-stuffed Genoa!"
"Good my liege!" Torel said, "it bore a scroll
Inscribed to Pavia, saying that I lived;
For in a year, a month, and day, not come,
I bade them hold me dead; and dead I am,
Albeit living, if my lady wed,
Perchance constrained." "Certes," spake Saladin,
"A noble dame—the like not won, once lost—
How many days remain?" "Ten days, my prince,
And twelvescore leagues between my heart and
me:
Alas! how to be passed?" Then Saladin—
"Lo! I am loath to lose thee—wilt thou swear
To come again if all go well with thee,
Or come ill speeding?" "Yea, I swear, my king,
Out of true love," quoth Torel, "heartfully."
Then Saladin, "Take here my signet-seal;
My admiral will loose his swiftest sail
Upon its sight; and cleave the seas, and go
And clip thy dame, and say the Trader sends
A gift, remindful of her courtesies."

Passed were the year, and month, and day; and passed
Out of all hearts but one Sir Torel's name,
Long given for dead by ransomed Pavians:
For Pavia, thoughtless of her Eastern graves,
A lovely widow, much too gay for grief,
Made peals from half a hundred campaniles
To ring a wedding in. The seven bells
Of San Pietro, from the nones to noon,
Boomed with bronze throats the happy tidings out;
Till the great tenor, overswelled with sound,
Cracked himself dumb. Thereat the sacristan,
Leading his swinkèd ringers down the stairs,
Came blinking into sunlight—all his keys
Jingling their little peal about his belt—
Whom, as he tarried, locking up the porch,
A foreign signor, browned with southern suns,
Turbaned and slippered, as the Muslims use,
Plucked by the cope. "Friend," quoth he—'twas a tongue
Italian true, but in a Muslim mouth—
"Why are your belfries busy—is it peace

Or victory, that so ye din the ears
Of Pavian lieges?" "Truly, no liege thou!"
Grunted the sacristan, "who knowest not
That Dame Adalieta weds to-night
Her fore-betrothed,—Sir Torel's widow she,
That died i' the chain?" "To-night!" the stranger said.
"Ay, sir, to-night!—why not to-night?—to-night!
And you shall see a goodly Christian feast
If so you pass their gates at even-song,
For all are asked."
No more the questioner,
But folded o'er his face the Eastern hood,
Lest idle eyes should mark how idle words
Had struck him home. "So quite forgot!—so soon!—
And this the square wherein I gave the joust,
And that the loggia, where I fed the poor;
And yon my palace, where—oh, fair! oh, false!—
They robe her for a bridal. Can it be?
Clean out of heart, with twice six flying moons,
The heart that beat on mine as it would break,

That faltered forty oaths. Forced! forced!—not false—
Well! I will sit, wife, at thy wedding-feast,
And let mine eyes give my fond faith the lie."

So in the stream of gallant guests that flowed
Feastward at eve, went Torel; passed with them
The outer gates, crossed the great courts with them,
A stranger in the walls that called him lord.
Cressets and coloured lamps made the way bright,
And rose-leaves strewed to where within the doors
The master of the feast, the bridegroom, stood,
A-glitter from his forehead to his foot,
Speaking fair welcomes. He, a courtly lord,
Marking the Eastern guest, bespoke him fair,
Prayed place for him, and bade them set his seat
Upon the dais. Then the feast began,
And wine went free as wit, and music died—
Outdone by merrier laughter:—only one
Nor ate nor drank, nor spoke nor smiled; but gazed
On the pale bride, pale as her crown of pearls,
Who sate so cold and still, and sad of cheer,
At the bride-feast.

But of a truth, Torel

Read the thoughts right that held her eyelids down,
And knew her loyal to her memories.
Then to a little page who bore the wine,
He spake, "Go tell thy lady thus from me:
In mine own land, if any stranger sit
A wedding-guest, the bride, out of her grace,
In token that she knows her guest's good-will,
In token she repays it, brims a cup,
Wherefrom he drinking she in turn doth drink;
So is our use." The little page made speed
And told the message. Then that lady pale—
Ever a gentle and a courteous heart—
Lifted her troubled eyes and smiled consent
On the swart stranger. By her side, untouched,
Stood the brimmed gold; "Bear this," she said, "and pray
He hold a Christian lady apt to learn
A kindly lesson." But Sir Torel loosed
From off his finger—never loosed before—
The ring she gave him on the parting day;
And ere he drank, behind his veil of beard
Dropped in the cup the ruby, quaffed, and sent.—

Then she, with sad smile, set her lips to drink,
And—something in the Cyprus touching them,
Glanced—gazed—the ring!—her ring!—Jove! how
 she eyes
The wistful eyes of Torel!—how, heartsure,
Under all guise knowing her lord returned,
She springs to meet him coming!—telling all
In one great cry of joy.
 O me! the rout,
The storm of questions! stilled, when Torel spake
His name, and, known of all, claimed the Bride Wife,
Maugre the wasted feast, and woful groom.
All hearts but his were light to see Torel;
But Adalieta's lightest, as she plucked
The bridal-veil away. Something therein—
A lady's dagger—small, and bright, and fine—
Clashed out upon the marble. "Wherefore that?"
Asked Torel; answered she, "I knew you true;
And I could live, so long as I might wait;
But they—they pressed me hard! my days of grace
Ended to-night—and I had ended too,
Faithful to death, if so thou hadst not come."

THE RAJAH'S RIDE.

A PUNJAB SONG.

Now is the Devil-horse come to Sindh!
  Wah! wah! gooroo!—that is true!
His belly is stuffed with the fire and the wind,
  But a fleeter steed had Runjeet Dehu!

It's forty koss from Lahore to the ford,
  Forty and more to far Jummoo;
Fast may go the Feringhee lord,
  But never so fast as Runjeet Dehu!

Runjeet Dehu was King of the Hill,
  Lord and eagle of every crest;
Now the swords and the spears are still,
  God will have it—and God knows best!

Rajah Runjeet sate in the sky,
  Watching the loaded Kafilas in;
Affghan, Kashmeree, passing by,
  Paid him pushm to save their skin.

Once he caracoled into the plain,
  Wah! the sparkle of steel on steel!
And up the pass came singing again
  With a lakh of silver borne at his heel.

Once he trusted the Mussulman's word,
  Wah! wah! trust a liar to lie!
Down from his eyrie they tempted my Bird,
  And clipped his wings that he could not fly.

Fettered him fast in far Lahore,
  Fast by the gate at the Runchenee Pul;
Sad was the soul of Chunda Kour,
  Glad the merchants of fat Kurnool.

Ten months Runjeet lay in Lahore—
  Wah! a hero's heart is brass!
Ten months never did Chunda Kour
  Braid her hair at the tiring-glass.

There came a steed from Toorkistan,
  Wah! God made him to match the hawk!
Fast beside him the four grooms ran,
  To keep abreast of the Toorkman's walk.

Black as the bear on Iskardoo;
  Savage at heart as a tiger chained;
Fleeter than hawk that ever flew,
  Never a Muslim could ride him reined.

"Runjeet Dehu! come forth from thy hold"—
  Wah! ten months had rusted his chain!
"Ride this Sheitan's liver cold"—
  Runjeet twisted his hand in the mane.

Runjeet sprang to the Toorkman's back,
  Wah! a king on a kingly throne!
Snort, black Sheitan! till nostrils crack,
  Rajah Runjeet sits, a stone.

Three times round the Maidan he rode,
  Touched its neck at the Kashmiree wall,
Struck the spurs till they spirted blood,
  Leapt the rampart before them all!

Breasted the waves of the blue Ravee,
  Forty horsemen mounting behind,
Forty bridle-chains flung free,—
  Wah! wah! better chase the wind!

Chunda Kour sate sad in Jummoo :—
  Hark! what horse-hoof echoes without?
"Rise! and welcome Runjeet Dehu—
  Wash the Toorkman's nostrils out!

"Forty koss he has come, my life!
  Forty koss back he must carry me;
Rajah Runjeet visits his wife,
  He steals no steed like an Afreedee.

"They bade me teach them how to ride—
  Wah! wah! now I have taught them well!"
Chunda Kour sank low at his side!
  Rajah Runjeet rode the hill.

When he came back to far Lahore—
  Long or ever the night began—
Spake he, "Take your horse once more,
  He carries well—when he bears a man."

Then they gave him a khillut and gold,
  All for his honour and grace and truth;
Sent him back to his mountain-hold—
  Muslim manners have touch of ruth.

Sent him back, with dances and drum—
  Wah! my Rajah Runjeet Dehu!
To Chunda Kour and his Jummoo home—
  Wah! wah! futtee!—wah, gooroo!

THE CALIPH'S DRAUGHT.

UPON a day in Ramadan—
  When sunset brought an end of fast,
And in his station every man
  Prepared to share the glad repast—
Sate Mohtasim in royal state,
  The pillaw smoked upon the gold;
The fairest slave of those that wait
  Mohtasim's jewelled cup did hold.

Of crystal carven was the cup,
  With turquoise set along the brim,
A lid of amber closed it up;
  'Twas a great king that gave it him.
The slave poured sherbet to the brink,
  Stirred in wild honey and pomegranate,
With snow and rose-leaves cooled the drink,
  And bore it where the Caliph sate.

The Caliph's mouth was dry as bone,
He swept his beard aside to quaff:—
The news-reader beneath the throne,
Went droning on with *ghain* and *kaf*.—
The Caliph drew a mighty breath,
Just then the reader read a word—
And Mohtasim, as grim as death,
Set down the cup and snatched his sword.

"*Ann' amratan shureefatee!*"
"Speak clear!" cries angry Mohtasim;
"*Fe lasr ind' ilj min ulji*,"—
Trembling the newsman read to him
How in Ammoria, far from home,
An Arab girl of noble race
Was captive to a lord of Roum;
And how he smote her on the face,

And how she cried, for life afraid,
"Ya, Mohtasim! help, O my king!"
And how the Kafir mocked the maid,
And laughed, and spake a bitter thing,

"Call louder, fool! Mohtasim's ears
Are long as Barak's—if he heed—
Your prophet's ass; and when he hears,
He'll come upon a spotted steed!"

The Caliph's face was stern and red,
He snapped the lid upon the cup;
"Keep this same sherbet, slave," he said,
"Till such time as I drink it up.
Wallah! the stream my drink shall be,
My hollowed palm my only bowl,
Till I have set this lady free,
And seen that Roumi dog's head roll."

At dawn the drums of war were beat,
Proclaiming, "Thus saith Mohtasim,
'Let all my valiant horsemen meet,
And every soldier bring with him
A spotted steed.'" So rode they forth,
A sight of marvel and of fear;
Pied horses prancing fiercely north,
Three lakhs—the cup borne in the rear!

When to Ammoria he did win,
  He smote and drove the dogs of Roum,
And rode his spotted stallion in,
  Crying, "*Labbayki!* I am come!"
Then downward from her prison-place
  Joyful the Arab lady came;
She held her hair before her face,
  She kissed his feet, she called his name.

She pointed where that lord was laid:
  They drew him forth, he whined for grace:
Then with fierce eyes Mohtasim said—
  "She whom thou smotest on the face
Had scorn, because she called her king:
  Lo! he is come! and dost thou think
To live, who didst this bitter thing
  While Mohtasim at peace did drink?"

Flashed the fierce sword—rolled the lord's head;
  The wicked blood smoked in the sand.
"Now bring my cup!" the Caliph said.
  Lightly he took it in his hand,

As down his throat the sweet drink ran
  Mohtasim in his saddle laughed,
And cried, "*T'aba asshrab alan!*
  Wallah! delicious is this draught!"

THE END.